Crossing with the Virgin

Virgin of Guadalupe tapestry hangs on border wall in Nogales, Sonora.

Crossing with the Virgin

STORIES FROM THE MIGRANT TRAIL

BY ~
KATHRYN FERGUSON,
NORMA A. PRICE,
AND TED PARKS

with forewords by
Claudia Aburto Guzmán
and Rev. John M. Fife

The University of Arizona Press   Tucson

The University of Arizona Press

www.uapress.arizona.edu

Library of Congress Cataloging-in-Publication Data
Ferguson, Kathryn.
Crossing with the Virgin : stories from the migrant trail / Kathryn Ferguson,
Norma A. Price, and Ted Parks ; with forewords by John M. Fife and
Claudia Aburto Guzmán.
p. cm.
Includes bibliographical references.
ISBN 978-0-8165-2854-7 (pbk. : alk. paper)
1. Illegal aliens—Mexican-American Border Region. 2. Humanitarian assistance—
Mexican-American Border Region. 3. Border crossing—Mexican-American Border
Region. 4. United States—Emigration and immigration—Social aspects. 5. Mexico—
Emigration and immigration—Social aspects. I. Price, Norma A., 1942– II. Parks, Ted,
1955– III. Title.
HV4011.M58F47 2010
304.8′730720922–dc22   2009033458

♻

Manufactured in the United States of America on acid-free,
archival-quality paper containing a minimum of 30% post-consumer
waste and processed chlorine free.

15 14 13 12 11 10   6 5 4 3

Our book is dedicated to migrants crossing through the southern Arizona desert, and to the families left behind. The stories were told to us by migrants we met on the trails and in the hospital between the years 2002 and 2008. We asked people if we could write their stories, and we kept notes on what they told us, including facts and feelings. We have changed names to keep people anonymous.

With Special Thanks

The publication of this book was generously supported by

Greg and Bonnie Kuykendall
H. Ray McPhail
Anne Patton
James D. Philips Jr.
Elizabeth Turner

Contents

List of Illustrations   xi

Acknowledgments   xiii

Foreword   xv
Claudia Aburto Guzmán

Foreword   xix
Rev. John M. Fife

DISCOVERING THE MIGRANT TRAIL

Volunteer   1
Ted Parks

First Samaritan Patrol   6
Norma Price

It's Personal   10
Kathryn Ferguson

STORIES FROM THE MIGRANT TRAIL

Story One   17
Norma

Story Two   21
Kathryn

Story Three   22
Norma

Story Four   26
Kathryn

Story Five   33
Ted

Story Six   36
Kathryn

Story Seven   44
Norma

Story Eight   48
Kathryn

Story Nine   52
Ted

Story Ten   56
Ted

NORMA
Story Eleven   63
Story Twelve   67
Story Thirteen   69
Story Fourteen   74

TED
Story Fifteen   81
Story Sixteen   86
Story Seventeen   91

KATHRYN
Story Eighteen   99
Story Nineteen   111
Story Twenty   117
Story Twenty-one   121
Story Twenty-two   127

TED
Story Twenty-three   131
Story Twenty-four   133
Story Twenty-five   136

NORMA

Story Twenty-six   141
Story Twenty-seven   146
Story Twenty-eight   149
Story Twenty-nine   151

KATHRYN

Story Thirty   159
Story Thirty-one   161
Story Thirty-two   167
Story Thirty-three   171

NORMA

Story Thirty-four   177
Story Thirty-five   183
Story Thirty-six   187

TED

Story Thirty-seven   193
Story Thirty-eight   199
Story Thirty-nine   201

Homage   205
Kathryn

Epilogue   207

Further Reading and Resources   209

Illustrations

Photographs

Virgin of Guadalupe tapestry on border wall
in Nogales, Sonora   ii
Three men pause to rest   15
Virgin of Guadalupe at a Tucson church   16
Kathryn Ferguson and Rabbi talk with migrants   29
Group waits in wash for pickup by their coyote   32
Crosses on border wall represent migrant deaths near Tucson   61
Migrants return to Mexico after release from custody   71
Crucifix near Sasabe, Mexico, looking north toward
Baboquivari Peak   79
A volunteer provides aid to migrants   90
Man rides freight train north   97
Migrants pass this painted image near Nogales, Sonora   101
Treatment of Carlos's amputated foot   110
Man climbs into "dog catcher" vehicle after apprehension   129
Veronica's baptism   139
Child's drawing found on trail in desert   149
Virgin of Guadalupe painted on rock wall near
Nogales, Sonora   157
Migrant belongings left at pickup site   164
Men apprehended by Border Patrol at Amado, Arizona   166
Border Patrol transfers detainees to Homeland Security bus   166
Foot mangled from train injury   175
Group waiting for their guide   186
Blistered feet from walking in desert   189
View of border wall from Nogales, Mexico   191
A pickup full of migrants heads toward the border   195
Cross memorializing death of sixty-four-year-old migrant   204
Tin art on Mexico side of border wall   206

Maps

Death map of southern Arizona   xiv
Historical map of Mexico prior to 1848   xviii
Southern Arizona, showing region of Samaritans' activities   xxiv

Acknowledgments

Many people have contributed to this collection of stories. It would be impossible to list them all, but we are grateful to those unnamed as well as the ones mentioned here. Justin Colussy-Estes was of paramount importance in editing Norma's stories, Gregory McNamee edited the first version of the manuscript, and Stephen Romaniello edited photographs. Thanks to Moses Thompson and Dr. John F. Chamblee, who provided maps. Margo Cowan, Bill Walker, Guadalupe Castillo, and John Fife were helpful in reviewing the manuscript for accuracy and providing advice. Gabriela Moreno-Alvarez helped with translation.

Many Samaritans shared stories, support, and encouragement, and our thanks goes out to each one, especially Sarah Roberts, Maria Ochoa, Helen Lundgren, Tracy Carroll, Dr. Antonio Zapien, and Faline Harshbarger.

Dr. Harvey Weiss provided medical information and shared his family's story. Dr. Joseph Price was helpful with encouragement and advice, and Dr. John Patton reviewed some medical descriptions. Each of us is indebted to family and special friends who supported us during this long process: Annalee and Gregory Gault, Santiago Jim Barnaby, and Karen Brennan for their support, translations, suggestions, and patience; Greg and Bonnie Kuykendall for their love and generosity; and many thanks to Stan Windham for his support.

We appreciate the unending work of all humanitarian groups working in southern Arizona: Green Valley Samaritans, No More Deaths, Humane Borders, Derechos Humanos, Border Action Network, BorderLinks, and all people dedicated to saving lives in the borderlands. Special thanks to Byrd Baylor for her encouragement to us as we began this project and for her many years of compassionate aid to those crossing through her desert home.

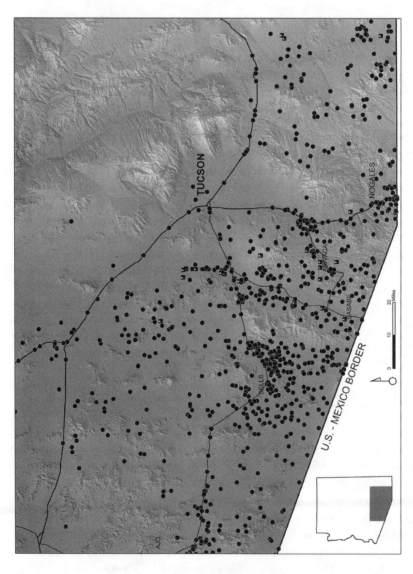

Death map of southern Arizona. Between October 1, 1999, and September 30, 2007, the U.S. Border Patrol recorded 1,138 deaths in southern Arizona. This map shows 906 deaths. Some locations indicate more than one death. (Courtesy of Humane Borders; cartographer: John F. Chamblee)

⚝⚝ ⚝⚝

Foreword

The hospitality of the Southwest with its wide open spaces and quaint, white-washed adobe brick towns is a myth. From its inception in the "American" national discourse this has been a contested territory. Here the relationship of power that exists between the United States and Mexico gets played out on a daily basis, a quotidian push and pull that encompasses all those who make this region their home. Southwest culture, founded on a Spanish, Mexican, and Native American core, is repeatedly tensioned by border politics, thereby generating economic, political, and environmental repercussions. These repercussions continue to present an ethical and moral challenge to those that live in the territory.

Much has been said about the Southwest being a third country, a *borderlands* that generates a hybrid culture rich in traditions and innovations. It is a place where the ancillary territory of the once colonial center of New Spain (now Mexico City) was swallowed by the ideology of Manifest Destiny, riding the crest of capitalist expansion. It is a place where each subsequent group has appropriated the previous group's culture, modified it, and added its own idiosyncrasies. Each cultural mutation has showcased the dominant dwellers' system of values, thrusting the previous system into "history," which, until recently, was understood as a timeline toward a prescribed concept of progress. As a result, the understanding of borderlands, this "unique" intermingling of cultures, rests on a process of erasure, denial, and distortion.

It might be difficult to believe or even consciously accept that this power relation has determined what we may or may not notice. Moreover, what we may or may not value as worth noticing. Mexican cuisine, Talavera pottery from Puebla, Mariachi music during a fire-lit southwestern sunset—these are things we enjoy. We value them as part of the romanticized notion we inscribe in concepts such as *hybrid culture* or *third country*. Yet, these are manifestations of a culture that has been subordinated and modified, to the extent that the struggle of those who generated the above commodities is now naturalized against the landscape and thereby erased from our ethical and moral compass.

The Southwest has its symbols that romance us as we go about our daily business in cities such as Phoenix, Albuquerque, Tucson, Santa Fe, and so on. It also has stories that reveal the effects of the relationship of power between the United States and the countries south of the political line. Stories such as the ones found here take place in what the Department of Homeland Security calls the Tucson Sector, named after the rapidly sprawling city of Tucson. This sector stretches from the New Mexico and Arizona state line to Yuma County in western Arizona for a total of 262 miles. Along the political national borderline we find small towns, usually with a counterpart on the other side of the border, that are surrounded by unpopulated arduous and treacherous terrain. During the summer it can reach 115 degrees Fahrenheit at midday; in the winter the night temperature may drop to below freezing. Both the vegetation and the fauna are hardy, having evolved in specific ways to survive in this ecosystem.

Owing to its geographical characteristics, its extreme temperatures, and its isolated stretches, this sector was thought of as a natural barrier to the northern border. It was to protect the United States against those whose livelihood fell into peril, detrimentally impacted by free-trade policies that favored large, well-equipped, U.S. government–subsidized farmers. This serious miscalculation on the extent and depth of the impact of contemporary policies on developing countries has led to a mass movement of peoples from diverse walks of life. The first waves of migration underscored the plight of the small farmer and laborer, who were first to be undercut by large U.S. growers of corn and other staples. However, four thousand known deaths as of 2007, and the various types of data collected by the active humanitarian groups at the border, demonstrate that not only have the migrant ethnic groups crossing the border diversified to include Guatemalan and Salvadorean ethnicities, but so have the class strata, as more professionals and middle-class individuals risk their lives in the desert crossing.

In the quotidian sphere of those who live in this sector, media obfuscate the ethical and moral dilemmas generated by the causal ramifications of irresponsible economic policies and the proximity to the political line. By sidestepping causality, ignoring the relationship of power and policies that have been put into effect, the individuals crossing the border are objectified, stereotyped, and as a result victimized. Nevertheless, there are fearless and compassionate citizens dwelling in the desert that acknowledge the cost of maintaining a "ready-made" culture, a prepackaged culture that is disconnected from the process and impact of production. They address the ethical and moral questions that beg to be asked in light of the mass migrations taking place.

The stories found in this collection are experiences lived by migrants, recounted through the lens of citizens who have chosen to grapple with the responsibility that living on the powerful side of a power relationship demands. The three authors here represented are members of one of the humanitarian groups that directly engage migrant lives. As members of the Samaritans, they hike or drive the desert trails and roads in hopes of preventing the death of a lost or abandoned migrant. They offer water, food, and medical assistance. Offerings such as these are contested by the law and by the dominant stance that has criminalized the travelers by erasing the migrants' stories and silencing the transformative, revelatory impact that an encounter in the desert has for the volunteers.

These stories not only offer a window to the migrants' plight, but also a view to the individual volunteers' own humanizing process. Each according to their profession, sensibility, and understanding of the "other," the human being that they are not, writes what she or he has encountered, the exchanges they have had, leading readers toward a greater understanding of their own responses to the moral and ethical coordinates in question. Whether in the field or a forensic lab, these writers attempt to give an account of what takes place on a daily basis in these borderlands. By using their own voices they give us a cross section of citizens who grapple with and act according to their causal responsibility, concretizing transformative human experiences. In these stories we find the blueprint for a different way of responding to and interacting with individuals who have always and already been part of our lives, as they are the ones who make our ready-made culture possible.

The lyrical voice of Kathryn Ferguson, the medical perspective given by Dr. Norma Price, the long-distance lens used by Ted Parks to narrate his stories, all give the reader the opportunity to reframe her or his responses to a situation that cannot be ignored, as we have a leading role in the unfolding drama. The stories found in these pages are not only about those "others" whom we read about in the newspaper and watch being arrested in the news; they are also about us, and how we are willing to reset our ethical and moral compass so as to no longer live in the shadow of those suffering in order to keep our houses comfortable.

—Claudia Aburto Guzmán, PhD
    Bates College

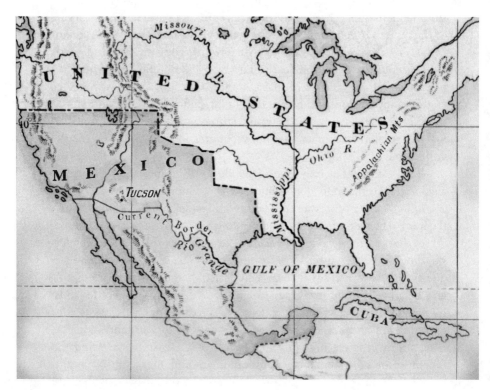

Historical map of Mexico prior to 1848. (Courtesy of Moses Thompson)

Foreword

I will tell you something about stories,
[he said]
They aren't just entertainment.
Don't be fooled.
They are all we have, you see,
all we have to fight off
illness and death.

You don't have anything
if you don't have the stories.
—LESLIE MARMON SILKO, CEREMONY

Every year for a decade, hundreds of people have died agonizing deaths as they have struggled to cross the desert of Arizona, risking everything to find jobs or join families. In *Crossing With the Virgin: Stories from the Migrant Trail*, three Samaritans relate stories told to them by people they have met on the migrant trails winding through mountains and canyons of the Sonoran Desert.

Samaritans is a humanitarian aid organization formed to save as many lives as possible in the deadly desert by providing food, water, and emergency medical care. This book tells the personal stories of migrants' journeys to the border, the hazards of crossing the line, and the desperate economic conditions that cause them to leave Mexico and Central America. Leaving home in search of an uncertain future, people often travel with an image of the Virgin of Guadalupe, putting their faith and their fate in her hands.

Stories are all we have to fight off the illness and death created by a tragically failed border enforcement policy. In the early 1980s we learned the wisdom of the Native American elder that Leslie Marmon Silko writes about. We learned to tell the stories. Back then, the human rights crisis on the border was the failure of the U.S. government to recognize as refugees people fleeing the death squads of El Salvador and the massacres of entire villages in Guatemala. The result was the capture and deportation of tens of thousands of terrified refugees.

Churches and synagogues, determined to defend human rights and U.S. refugee law, began to declare their houses of worship a "sanctuary" for refugee families. The first was Southside Presbyterian Church in Tucson, Arizona. By 1986 some 567 churches and synagogues had declared sanctuary and protected a refugee family. A new "underground railroad" had formed, moving refugees from the Southwest borderlands across the United States. Seventeen cities had voted to become "cities of sanctuary."

After eight years of struggle and over twenty federal court trials, an agreement was reached between the Justice Department and the Sanctuary movement. All deportations to El Salvador and Guatemala were ended, and refugees from those countries were given temporary protected status. We also learned a most valuable lesson over those eight years. The most effective and transforming factor was the stories of the refugees.

The Sanctuary movement prevailed against the power and the popularity of the Reagan administration, and against criminal indictments and prison sentences for Sanctuary workers. It prevailed because of the power of refugee stories. When a woman from El Salvador told her agonizing story of watching the army drag her husband from their home to be shot, and then being forced to watch their daughter being gang-raped, congregations, cities, courtrooms, and finally Congress were persuaded. The policy changed because of the stories.

Now a new crisis of human rights violations, death, and suffering has devastated the borderlands. Once again people of conscience and faith are struggling to save lives. Once again the U.S. government is declared to be in violation of international law. Once again the voices of fear and bigotry are dominating the public discourse. The silence of the migrant voice and the absence of their stories are the reasons for this book. We won't have anything if we don't have the stories.

To understand the context for these stories, an understanding of the history of the border is crucial. The current border between the United States and Mexico was determined as a result of the Mexican-American War in 1848. In Mexico, they call it "La Invasión Yanqui." The United States acquired what are now California, Nevada, Arizona, Utah, New Mexico, and Texas.

The U.S. Border Patrol was not established until 1924. Its primary mission during Prohibition was to keep contraband whiskey from crossing. Then, in the depths of the Great Depression, the border enforcement became serious. Anyone of Mexican descent (whether or not a U.S. citizen) was rounded up and deported at gunpoint.

The border opened up again during World War II when migrant workers from Mexico were desperately needed in the fields and war industries. This economic need was recognized by an agreement between the U.S. and Mexican governments in 1942 called the "Bracero Program." Each year hundreds of thousands of migrant workers were given a temporary visa to cross to work. The program was ended in 1964 under pressure from the AFL-CIO, but the reality remained. The United States had become dependent on that cheap source of labor in expanding sectors of the economy. Thus the ambivalence that has marked border policy ever since was established.

Unauthorized migrant workers, who needed the jobs, continued to cross the border to work, fulfilling the U.S. demand for labor. Three-fourths returned permanently to Mexico, but those remaining were periodically granted documents recognizing their status as permanent residents. A registry for undocumented families was granted in 1924, 1948, 1972, and finally in 1986 under President Reagan.

All that changed in 1994. Under political pressure to do something about "illegals," the Border Patrol adopted a new border enforcement strategy. The new strategy was simple and clear from government planning documents. Since almost all of the migration of workers occurred in the urban areas along the border, the first objective was to seal off those cities with steel fences, technology, and a dramatic increase in personnel. The plan anticipated that when the urban areas were secured, migrant workers would try to cross the border in isolated, hazardous, and wilderness areas. Planners believed that when word got out about how hazardous the crossing had become, this would become a deterrent. As the plan, called "Operation Gatekeeper," unfolded in the 1990s, the Border Patrol hoped that the isolated and deadly Sonoran Desert would be a "geographical barrier" to migration. Instead, the death toll set a new record each year, and Operation Gatekeeper became a strategy of deterrence by death. That is a violation of human rights and of international law according to a six-judge panel of the Inter-American Court of Human Rights. It is the context for the stories in this book.

One other critical factor needs to be understood as well. It is no coincidence that the walls started to go up in 1994, the same year that the North American Free Trade Agreement (NAFTA) was implemented. While it was publicly declared that NAFTA would "solve the immigration problem," the walls being built on the border told the real story of the impending economic disaster. Under the terms of NAFTA, Mexico was required to end all agricultural subsidies for corn, rice, and beans. Then Mexico was mandated to phase out all tariffs on agricultural imports from the United States and Canada. It sounds like free trade until you remember how extensively the government of the United States subsidizes agriculture and exports. The result is that corn, for example, is being exported to Mexico at 24 percent under the cost of production. The World Bank estimates that 1.5 million small Mexican farmers were driven off the land by 2003, and that the total has now risen to 3.5 million.

So, once again, faith communities and people of conscience in the borderlands have been organizing to save lives in the desert. Humane Borders was organized in 2000 to place water stations in the critical areas where migrant bodies were being found. Each year, between twenty and twenty-five thousand gallons of water have been used by migrants.

Two years later, in 2002, Samaritans was organized to put four-wheel-drive vehicles on remote back roads. Volunteer doctors, nurses, and EMTs, accompanied by other Spanish speakers, take food, water, and emergency medical gear to the desert each day. They have found hundreds upon hundreds of migrants suffering from heatstroke, broken limbs, twisted joints, rattlesnake bites, heart attacks, and stroke. They have discovered the victims of rape and beatings, the lost and abandoned. Only the Virgin of Guadalupe knows how many lives have been saved.

Three of those Samaritans have written the stories of the men, women, and children they have encountered along the migrant trail. These stories are all that we have to fight off the illness and death in the desert.

Read these stories—then act to change the policy.

—Rev. John M. Fife

*Discovering the
Migrant Trail*

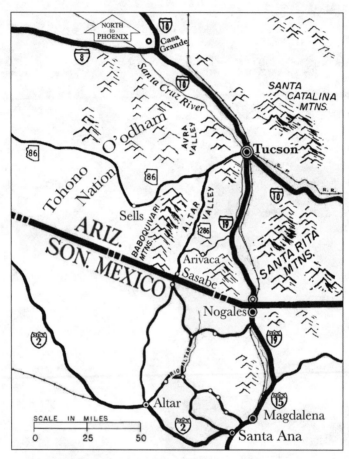

Map of southern Arizona showing region of Samaritans'
activities. (Courtesy of Moses Thompson)

Volunteer

~ TED

In the fall of 2005 a friend told me about a press conference being held at a church not far from my house. It had been called to publicize the plight of two young people volunteering for an organization called No More Deaths. They had been charged with crimes relating to their transporting three migrants in their vehicle to Tucson for medical care. The case had been getting a fair amount of publicity in the local newspapers. My understanding was that one of the three border crossers had bloody diarrhea for two days, and all suffered vomiting, severe dehydration, and blisters on their feet. The pair had been advised by medical staff to bring them into Tucson, since their condition was such that leaving them in the desert might be fatal.

Hundreds of people are found dead each year in the Tucson Sector of the U.S. Border Patrol, a 240-mile-long frontier that stretches from Lukeville, Arizona, to the New Mexico border. Almost all die from exposure to the elements. The area has vast expanses of uninhabited desert in which a person can become lost, die, and the body would never be found. Ever.

I could not understand why the U.S. government was wasting resources prosecuting people who, as I understood it, were only giving a ride to three men who needed medical care. Providing assistance to people in need of medical attention was now apparently a felony punishable by fifteen years in jail and a $500,000 fine. These people were not smugglers transporting migrants for the purpose of making money or for personal gain. I went to the press conference hoping some of these questions might be answered.

The press conference was being held in the sanctuary of a church. Inside there were more than a hundred people. Some lawyers for the organization No More Deaths were making speeches, and then they fielded questions from the media. I learned that one of the lawyers for the two defendants believed that their arrests had been a mistake. Rookie Border Patrol officers had made the bust, a new U.S. assistant attorney then filed charges, and now the government was stuck with an unpopular case that would end up being decided by a jury. The prosecutor had offered a generous plea bargain for the two defendants, but they had taken the high moral ground and would not accept it. With the rallying cry "Humanitarian Aid Is Never a Crime," this group was standing up for basic human rights and would not give up without a good fight.

As I was leaving the church, an acquaintance I had not seen in a while said hello and asked if I was interested in volunteering with a group called the Samaritans, who, she said, drove out into the desert each day and looked for people who were in need of food, water, and medical care. When I told her I might be interested, she informed me that a training session would be held on Sunday at the church and told me just to show up at the appointed time.

The following Sunday I arrived at the church in the afternoon. A number of people were milling about. We went into a meeting room and sat in a circle. There were about eleven of us; most were Christian Peace Maker team members from all over the United States and Canada. They were here as observers and were going to be deployed on the border to monitor the situation.

The meeting was very informal. A nurse gave us general information on what to look for in the field regarding medical issues, and a doctor gave us general guidelines as to what to do when we ran into these situations. We were told that Samaritans usually travel in groups of three: a medical person, a fluent Spanish speaker, and a third person called the "other" who is an observer.

The patrols, we learned, leave in the early morning in one of two four-wheel-drive vehicles the group owns, packed with water, food, and medical supplies. Bottled water is iced down during the summer months. The medical supplies consist of basics used to treat blisters on the feet and scrapes and sprains. There is also a baby bag with diapers and formula, since infants are encountered from time to time. The food packs are large plastic baggies filled with PowerBars or granola bars, tuna fish, or Vienna sausages, peanut butter crackers, and a candy bar. They are kept in the baggies so the Border Patrol can see what is in them. We were told that we can offer food and water to migrants in custody if the agent in charge allows it. When migrants are encountered in the field, we can administer to medical conditions, provide food and water, and, if they request, call the Border Patrol to have them returned to the border of their own volition. If the situation is immediately life threatening we can call the Border Patrol, and the medical arm of that organization, called BORSTAR, would respond.

A historian then gave us an overview of the history of the border. Tucson and a large swath of southern Arizona and New Mexico was a part of Mexico a little more than 150 years ago when the Gadsden Purchase of 1853 transferred thousands of square miles into the hands of the United States. To really understand the historical context of this fact requires one to shed the manifest destiny paradigm and come to face Mexicans as the dominant culture in this area.

The border along Arizona has always been a porous sieve through which families have crossed and recrossed many times looking for work and stray cattle, trading goods and services, and visiting relatives. The forces of commerce and the attendant human tide have created the need for an open border and have left it little more than an informal and arbitrary line dividing two governments. Depending on which way the political wind is blowing, the peoples who cross back and forth are always near the flash point for those who would use the race card for economic or political gain.

After the historian gave her lecture, one of the lawyers from the press conference talked about the legal issues involved with Samaritans. We were told that we couldn't transport migrants unless it was a matter of life and death. Apparently this is a new policy brought on by the arrest of the two in July. In the past the Border Patrol very seldom stopped Samaritans transporting migrants to the hospital for care and certainly would not arrest them. There had been an understanding with the previous head of the Tucson Sector of the Border Patrol regarding this issue. But now, in light of the arrest, we needed to be mindful of the consequences.

That afternoon I signed up for a patrol with my acquaintance and a doctor for later in the week. The day arrived, and at six in the morning we loaded up an SUV with supplies and set out west on Route 86 toward the Tohono O'odham Indian Nation. We slowed down after we passed Ryan Airfield and were driving at forty miles per hour, the preferred speed to conduct a patrol as the two passengers scan the desert for people. I was told they might be sitting, standing, or walking, and it would be easy to spot them at that slow speed.

We had been driving not five minutes at this slow speed when my two partners spotted a man walking east on the side of the road. He was carrying a plastic bag and appeared to me to be a guy walking to work, a man of Mexican descent but certainly not a migrant. We went past, and my partners said, "He's a migrant." We looked for a spot to make a

U-turn on the heavily trafficked highway. They decided that the Spanish speaker and I would make contact with him and assess his medical condition while the doctor drove the truck away, since parking may draw attention. The doctor would drive back and forth on the road, and we would flag her down if he needed medical care.

I thought that my partners were quite mistaken. Although the man was obviously Latino, he was not what I imagine migrants to look like, and he was on the main road into Tucson with lots of Border Patrol agents around. In fact, just as we were dropped off and began to walk toward the man, a Border Patrol agent zipped by. My partner asked the man in Spanish to step away from the road and sit down.

He seemed a bit disoriented to me, almost as if he had been drinking. The plastic bag had three bottles of Gatorade in it. My partner asked how long he had been walking in the desert.

"Four days."

"Are there any more in your party?"

"There were twenty, but we got split up." He didn't know where the rest of them were.

"Do you have any medical problems?"

"No. I'm just tired."

He told my partner that he had bought the Gatorade at the store down the way. She warned him that it is dangerous for him to walk on the road, since the Border Patrol comes by here all the time. As she said that, another cruiser blew by. I thought to myself, "Why don't they stop? Can't they see what these two civilians spotted easily enough?"

He asked us for a ride into Tucson. My partner told him that we couldn't give him one and warned him again that he would probably be picked up and deported back to Mexico if he continued to walk along this road. He seemed to understand, although he still looked confused and extremely tired and disoriented.

He asked how far away Tucson was and if it was on this road. She answered yes and said it was only ten kilometers away. She gave him her pack, which had food and water in it. He accepted it, and then he went under a barbed-wire fence and into the brush and disappeared.

Our ride returned, and we hopped in and continued down the road. I was amazed. He was not what I expected at all. My two companions let me know that you can never tell where or under what circumstances you will find migrants, nor what they will be doing, and they assured me that I would learn to spot them from afar.

We continued past Three Points and pulled off the road near a bridge that crosses a large arroyo. I was told we were going to hike in with packs and call out to migrants. We loaded up with supplies and dropped down into the wash and began walking. Our Spanish speaker began to call out, "Hola. Somos amigos de la iglesia. Tenemos agua, comida, y atención medica. No tengan miedo." (Hello. We are friends from the church. We have water, food, and medical help. Don't be afraid.) As we walked south, she called out continually, with only a few breaks to listen for a response.

We came across some footprints. My partners were familiar with tracking. They conferred and agreed the prints were only hours old. They appeared to be of five people, all headed north. We continued walking and soon came to a place where people had been resting and waiting to be picked up. They had left everything behind, and I was amazed at the amount of trash. It looked like an abandoned little campground with no fire pits from which the people were suddenly and mysteriously transported to another place. Hats, shoes, pants, shirts, backpacks, food, water bottles, toothbrushes, toothpaste, deodorant, coats, underwear, socks, large plastic garbage bags (used as sleeping bags and rain gear), and gloves were all spread out under the low-hanging branches of the mesquite and palo verde trees that lined the arroyo. Here they had rested before continuing the journey.

We walked for a while, crossed over to a small dry tributary of the arroyo, and headed back north toward our vehicle. The sun was beginning to stretch its rays into the bottom of the wash, and the heat felt good. We startled a barn owl, which soared down the wash, moving ahead of us, its silent wings huge against the blue sky.

We went back to the truck and drove south on Route 286, the mile markers counting off the distance to Mexico. We continued on at our snail's pace looking for those in need. At Arivaca Road we turned east, drove through rolling hills, and came upon a ribbon of green meandering into the small village of Arivaca, locally renowned as a center of methamphetamine production. We stopped for cookies at a bakery and continued our journey east past more barren rolling hills toward the Santa Rita Mountains and I-19, eventually turning north back to Tucson.

In the coming months I would learn this stretch of road. I would know it well enough to describe where the trails are near specific mile markers, where you can see wildlife, how far it is to good coffee and chilaquiles, where the Border Patrol likes to sit in the shade, and where the large potholes are in the road. I would learn that in this stretch of the world, where hungry people head north and die in the desert alone and far from home, a small group of individuals does what it can to alleviate the suffering of those they encounter on the migrant trails.

First Samaritan Patrol

~ Norma

No one disputes that southern Arizona is very hot. During the summer months the temperatures in the desert range from 105 to 115 degrees Fahrenheit. On the desert floor it can be 130 degrees or higher. It was June of 2002, the "dry-summer" season in the Sonoran Desert, and the hottest month of the year. Here in southern Arizona we have two types of summer, as designated by the Arizona-Sonora Desert Museum: Foresummer, or dry-summer, is the months of May and June with high temperatures, no rain, and very low humidity; then in July the Monsoon Summer arrives with almost daily afternoon rains and sudden thunderstorms punctuated by dramatic lightning displays.

My husband relaxed in a cozy chair reading the newspaper in the cool comfort of our home. We had already been for our daily hike in the early morning when it was cooler. Only in Arizona four years, we had quickly adopted a daily routine adjusted to the predictable searing midday temperatures of summer months.

For several years I had been volunteering in the Herpetology Department at the Arizona-Sonora Desert Museum. When I retired from medicine and moved to Tucson I was unsure how I would feel about leaving active practice, but I truly fell in love with the desert. For about eighteen months after retiring I had a gnawing sort of feeling about not working—I don't know if it was in the pit of my stomach or the back of my mind. Ever since I was sixteen years old there had never been an extended period of time that I wasn't working or in school. I had never been without a job. Certainly I had attacked school as if it were a job. Now, having left the practice of medicine, I filled my days as much as if I had been working: hiking, yoga, Spanish conversation classes, birding—even volunteering with a sparrow-banding project for several years. I was spending two days a week at the Desert Museum and was thoroughly captivated with that magical place. Fascinated with the lizards we were studying, I became absorbed in lizard behavior and classification, never caring that I had to begin at an early hour or bothered by the summer heat of the late morning and midday. Even though I was not getting a paycheck for my activities, I was having a wonderful time and was extremely busy. My daughter and son had said, "Mom, I think you are busier than you have ever been." Previously I had been available for their calls in the office, hospital, or clinic.

Now, after four years, I was comfortable with my lifestyle and enjoying the southern Arizona desert. Then my husband said, "Norma, can you find out about this?" As we sat in the comfort of our air-conditioned home, he held up a copy of the local weekly newspaper. The lead article reported on a group putting water in the desert for migrants crossing the Arizona-Mexico border and coming north for jobs.

"It is a crime," he said, "that these people who need jobs, whose labor is needed and even recruited, should have to risk their lives or even die, seeking a way to support their families. Remember Yolanda Gonzalez?" That story had captured everyone's attention when reported in the national news.

Nineteen-year-old Yolanda Gonzalez had died after giving her last drops of water to her eighteen-month-old baby girl. The toddler lived and was returned to her grandmother in Oaxaca, in southern Mexico. Yolanda was coming north to be with her husband, already working here, and to get a job herself to help support the family. CBS news reports cited the extreme poverty in the remote village where Yolanda had lived: a three-dollar wage for a day's work and jobs extremely scarce. Quoting Mexican officials, the reports said that for every five Mexicans looking for work there was only one job available.

Every time we read another news account of death in the desert, my husband said, "Surely there is some way that water can be put in the desert for those crossing through." Now he was holding up the newspaper that reported the activities of Humane Borders. That group put out fifty-five-gallon water tanks in specific locations in the desert and marked them with blue flags on thirty-foot poles so they could be seen from a distance. Stan said, "Norma, call and see what we can do to help."

The next Saturday the two of us joined a Humane Borders trip into the desert to set up a new water station near the community of Three Points, located between Tucson and the land belonging to the Tohono O'odham Nation. The water barrels were placed near a known route that migrant groups traveled as they headed north. We spent the whole day with Humane Borders checking and refilling water in the existing stations. We learned what they were doing to prevent deaths in the desert and gained a more in-depth knowledge of the complexity of border issues. We were told that a new group called Samaritans was having its first meeting and training session at Southside Presbyterian Church the following day. I knew I wanted to go.

That first meeting on Sunday afternoon, June 30, lasted almost seven hours. We took dishes for potluck supper, and after food and fellowship, we reconvened in the church sanctuary, the kiva, a space filled with inspiration and spiritual energy. After the long afternoon of information about border history and how Samaritans would function, the day ebbed to a contemplative and introspective close. Pastor John Fife, veteran of the Sanctuary movement, torchbearer of human rights and border justice, stood to ask for a moment of silence in thoughtful meditation for the first Samaritan patrol going out the following day. He named those who would be going on patrol: Matt, who had a four-wheel-drive vehicle, and Jody, who spoke Spanish. Then he said, "the medical patrol member is unable to go tomorrow and we need a medical person to complete the group. Is there someone who can go?"

No response.

"We really need a medical volunteer."

In that room of seventy people, there were sixty-eight whom I did not know; my husband was the only familiar face. I did not feel very bold.

Again John spoke, in a manner with which I would become familiar over the coming years. "Come on folks. Who will volunteer to go tomorrow?"

My hand shot up.

No questions asked, he just said, "Good, great. It's set then." I have never regretted one moment of my involvement with Samaritans. It has enriched my life in ways I could never have foreseen.

After that first day I would never have thought that Samaritans would still be patrolling the desert seven years later. At that time we were convinced that changes in immigration policy would be enacted, that workers from other countries would be able to enter our country without having to risk their lives, that families could be reunited without experiencing the death of a child or spouse. I was certain that today there would be no need for our presence in remote areas of the southern Arizona desert. I have been proven wrong.

The inaugural trip of Samaritans on the day following that first training is a vivid memory. We did not leave until noon because of a prior press conference at the church and blessing of the patrol vehicle by the Presbyterian minister and two Tohono O'odham women church members. Shaking water from greasewood branches, the women anointed the vehicle. The greasewood plant is a symbol of living and of eternal life. When the droughts come, it stays green longer than other desert plants.

We drove west on Highway 86 from Tucson across the Tohono O'odham Nation to Ajo, an old mining town 130 miles across the desert. On that first patrol the driver was Matt, a young man very instrumental in planning and beginning the organization of Samaritans. Jody and I scoured each side of the highway looking for people alone or in a group, walking through fields or down the road. Humane Borders had been active for over a year and told us they saw migrants in large groups, and alone. We expected to see people under trees and on the roadside. The vehicle we rode in belonged to Matt, but there was no air conditioning in his fifteen-year-old Isuzu Trooper, and at noon on July 1 it was a very hot trip. We encountered no migrants that day, although we drove at such a slow speed on the federal highway that traffic honked and passed us the entire drive to Ajo. Even though we returned to Tucson that July 1 evening not having seen one migrant, I felt convinced that this was an important mission. And now, all these years later, I have a profound commitment to this effort. I know that lives have been saved, deaths prevented, because of the work of humanitarian groups in the borderlands.

It's Personal

It was low, slow, and mournful. He dragged the scarlet notes across the floor like a velvet gown. I sat on the couch, next to two basset hounds, and listened to Bill play the trumpet. Light shined through the French doors where vines wrapped around panes of glass with orange and yellow flowers hand-painted by Angie. Bill was a musician. He played in the Army Air Corps Band with Zoot Sims, and later in Tucson he arranged charts for Louis Leon's Big Dance Band. It seemed the perfect life. When I got older, I would go to Gus and Andy's Steak House on Miracle Mile to hear Bill's jazz improvisations.

Some of my favorite childhood memories took place in the house of my godparents, Bill and Angie Eagle. My sister and I would go to the house to play with the kids, Jim and Chris. But my favorite moments were when Bill picked up that trumpet to practice.

I'll never forget the day Angie removed the curlers, combed through my hair, and we saw that it was pink. She tsk tsked, the clients exclaimed, but secretly I was proud. I wanted my hair color changed, but the pink was unplanned. Angie left the dye a little too long. When I went to my high school, I was the envy of all the girls. My mother and I often went to Angie's Beauty Shop on Grande in Tucson. The shop was always busy. I remember listening to the beautiful Spanish language all the women spoke. I learned a few words but was too shy to say much. I think I was the shop mascot because I was allowed to just be there as Angie bustled around, chatting with her clients.

Hanging out on Grande with my Mexican American godparents was one of the best memories of my life. They taught me the first Spanish words I learned, but mostly I just had fun with them. It wouldn't be until many years later that I realized they were a major reason I joined Samaritans to help in the desert. It was because of my relationship to them and because of life-changing experiences in the Sierra Madre in Chihuahua, Mexico. For the last fifteen years, I have come and gone from the Sierra while making documentaries as an independent filmmaker.

Partly because of its astounding beauty and ruggedness, but mostly because I have friends in Choguita and Norogachi in the Barranca del Cobre (Copper Canyon), I fell in love with the Sierra. I was born in Arizona but feel that I am going home to the Sierra.

My friends are serious country people—small-ranch owners and *arrieros* (muleteers) of the most elegant kind. You may think to call a muleteer "elegant" is a bad choice of words, but they are nothing less. They are the essence of remaining Mestizo culture.

To ride with Hiram Loya Villalobos on horseback to the high country to tend his cornfield, returning along the riverbanks in a snowstorm, cutting through a rainbow and arriving back at his kitchen in time for his wife, Elia, to dish out steaming *frijoles de olla* is sublime.

Hiram, handsome and intelligent, has outwitted a twenty-year drought by working dawn to dusk, caring for crops, family, and animals. He takes people on pack trips through the most traditional Tarahumara backcountry to the upper Rio Conchos for Matachin dances and peyote healing ceremonies. But this is not regular tourist fare. We're talking about thirty-five-day pack trips with mules where you have to be experienced and smart, or you won't find your way home. The Sierra is generous but unforgiving.

Next to Hiram's hand-built adobe house is the *bodega* (storehouse) and *potrero* (corral). It's the kind of place *Architectural Digest* dreams of profiling in a photo-essay that depicts a "rustic" home, and lifestyle. But what's missing in the magazine is sweat and the smell of saddle oil. You open a shutter to pull out a rebuilt Tejano saddle, the worn hide glistening, as comfortable as your favorite leather chair at home. It is a saddle with *hombros* (shoulders), which allow the rider to position the legs so he is not fighting to stay in the saddle while riding down a narrow mountain trail knocking against thick brush. It comes with *tapaderas* (which look like a monkey's head) into which you put your feet to keep them away from brush. Beside the saddles hang *reatas* and *frenos*, beautiful braided leather ropes and bits used to control the animals.

About a mile up the hill from Hiram's, on a slab of white rock, is the house of Ernesto Diaz Holguin, his wife, Pascola, and his ten children. His adobe house is covered with pine shakes made by hand long ago. The shakes are illegal now because they require old growth pine. Until recently, water was hand carried up the steep hill from the stream below. Near his house is his small store stocked with *fideo*, cans of tuna, *maseca*, cheese, and a few household goods. But sales are few because no one in Norogachi has money. Drought becomes a way of life.

Ernesto and Gabriel Molina Garcia took me, a photographer friend, Susie, and two burros into the Tarahumara backcountry to help me film a documentary. It was a five-day walk in July. Imelda, Gabriel's wife, prepared tortillas, frijoles, and chiles to last us a couple of days. On the first day, Ernesto and Gabriel, wearing Levi's, plaid shirts, white vaquero hats, and huaraches, packed up the burros and we headed off. Since none of us knew each other well, we were quiet and infinitely polite. Susie and I walked behind the men. They kept turning around to make sure we were okay.

As the day wore on and the dust thickened, they started whispering and laughing. We stopped late in the afternoon to make camp. They cleared the ground for a fire and fussed at length over the proper spot where we would lay our sleeping bags, gleefully bustling around, joking about everything, acting as if it were boys' night out. We came to find out it was. They weren't accustomed to packing gringos, much less two unaccompanied women. After we ate, Gabriel dumped laurel leaves into boiling water for tea. Ernesto sat down on his heels Tarahumara style by the fire, took off his hat, and politely held it in his hand. He still wore his 1950s Hollywood silver-frame sunglasses. Somehow I knew we were about to have a heart-to-heart.

"Mira . . . tenemos una pregunta." Look, we have a question. "¿Porque estan solas aquí por el campo? ¿No saben que es peligroso aquí? ¿Donde estan los hombres?" Why are you here alone in the countryside. Don't you know it's dangerous? Where are your men? All day they had been dying to ask.

Until then, I hadn't thought about it. But by the end of the evening, I felt sorry for myself, had deeply examined my life, and wondered the same thing. Maybe they were right. Where are the men?! It was like a Woody Allen movie. Ernesto and Gabriel couldn't understand why we would be traveling without husbands. Although Susie explained that she had a nice one at home, they couldn't understand why he had let her come alone. I said she's not alone, she is with us. It's not the same, they said. Then they asked why I wasn't married. I said I had been, but presently wasn't. Ernesto said you should be. I said, but I'm not in love with anyone. He said love doesn't matter. You need someone to share the chores with. Before the night was over, we started to agree with them that perhaps we were missing something and should make our lives more like theirs, and they admitted that their wives were a little jealous and didn't want them guiding single gringas, but they were happy because it was really good to get out, take a little vacation (they didn't consider this work compared to their usual heavy labor), and maybe they should make their lives more like ours. After mere hours on the trail together, we were already old friends.

Ernesto would never consider crossing over to the United States. He likes his life. But his sons would. They want to help their family. We were sitting next to the goat pen when a son told me two of them were going to cross the desert to work. I told them not to cross, that it is dangerous.

Weeks later, when I returned to Tucson, I thought often about them. I felt that if Ernesto's boys did enter the desert and died out there, I would be responsible. It would be as if they had died in my front yard; I would never forgive myself. I had heard about increasing deaths on the desert but thought as an individual I could do nothing. Then I heard about the Samaritans volunteer organization and signed up.

Because of my childhood with my godparents in Tucson, and good friends in the Sierra, I had no choice but to get out there and help. It was personal. I grew up in the mixed culture of Tucson and was horrified that good people looking for work were dying merely to come here for minimum-wage jobs.

I would come to learn that not only very poor people were crossing the desert. We would also meet successful people who had fallen on bad financial times. We would meet people like my godparents who had strong businesses: naturopaths, shop owners, accountants, corporate executives, and bankers. We would meet funny, smart, hardworking ranchers and farmers like my friends in Norogachi.

Not everyone in Mexico is queuing up to come to the United States. But many are. Most people who come are in crisis. By the time we encounter them on the desert, they are not at their best. It is a serious and difficult decision to cross over. The border is a low-level war zone where there are men with guns—Border Patrol, National Guard, thieves, Minutemen, ranchers, hunters, helicopters, ATVs, horse patrols, and Humvees. And I am appalled that people like my godparents, whose family came here as immigrants, and that people like my friends in the Sierra, are treated inhumanely by people with guns, or that they die in the desert. Yes, it is personal.

Stories from the Migrant Trail

Photograph by Helen Lundgren

Virgin of Guadalupe at a Tucson church.

Previous page: Three men pause to rest.

Story One

~ Norma

I t has been four days since Día de la Virgen de Guadalupe, December 12, and the image of the Virgin at St. John's Catholic Church in Tucson is covered with flowers. One month ago I watched a parishioner with a paintbrush touching up the gold paint on the design imprinted on the Virgin's dress. I am standing outside of St. John's sanctuary in front of the gazebo that shelters the serene statue. It is crowded with flowers, some artificial, most real. The majority are roses: red, yellow, and an occasional white or pink. There is one pot of poinsettias and scattered other floral varieties. Over on one side are forty or fifty votive candles.

The features of this image are softer and more human than most I have seen of the Virgin of Guadalupe. The gentle brown face is framed by black hair, her eyes downcast, looking to one side. With dark eyebrows and eyes lined in black, her hazel-eyed gaze is unexpected. Her palms meet in front of her chest in a gesture of prayer. Draped over her hands are four withered roses that supplicants have placed in homage. The gold-bordered green robe is sprinkled with shiny, golden stars. On her head is a gold crown, studded with jewels and topped off by a withered red rose, gift of a devotee. The pink dress she wears has a design imprinted in gold, the same that was being refreshed by the artisan I watched a month ago. An aura of light surrounds the image: rays of gold and red. It is impossible to see the tiny angel or cherub below the Virgin because of so many flowers.

In 1531 the Virgin of Guadalupe revealed herself in a vision to an indigenous boy named Juan Diego. Because of her grace in choosing this humble peasant as her messenger to the bishop in Mexico City, the people of Mexico have long revered her as their patron saint. A lot of Mexican desert crossers give credit to her for their successful journey, for keeping them safe, for recovery after injury or illness, or escape from death. Many migrants wear amulets or jewelry bearing her image. In campsites where belongings have been left there is always her image emblazoned on T-shirts, caps, backpacks, and other mementos.

As I stand before the gazebo, I am impressed at how many of the flowers are still fresh, especially the roses. Roses are legendary in the Virgin's appearance to Juan Diego. When he reached Mexico City, he told the bishop that the Virgin had sent him with a message to build a church on the spot where she had appeared to him. Skeptical, the bishop told him to return home and bring back a sign from the Virgin. The young peasant returned to the rocky hills of Guadalupe. Again he prayed, and when she appeared he told the Virgin of the doubts and the request for proof. She instructed him to go to the rocky outcropping on top of the hill. There he saw roses growing from rocks and blooming in early December. She directed him to pick the flowers and take them to Mexico City. The young boy filled his *manta*, or robe, with as many roses as he could carry. When he arrived in the city and stood before the bishop, he unfolded his manta, and roses fell to the ground. There on the fabric of his robe was an image of the Virgin.

María Flores was confident of her protection by the Virgin. María was an attractive middle-aged woman, self-assured and independent. She had an enviable thick mane of hair, colored a dark auburn with light brown- and blond-streaked highlights. Her left foot and ankle were in a half-cast, temporary immobilization until her appointment with an orthopedist. Both of the bones in her lower leg were broken. She had stumbled and fallen, unable to keep pace with the rest of her group. When it became impossible to bear weight on her left leg, and she was unable to continue, the *pollero* and group left her behind. But her nephew stayed at her side, unwilling to leave her to struggle alone, even knowing he would be returned to Mexico.

María came from a suburb of Mexico City. She made fifty dollars a week selling phone cards. She had four adult children, but even living alone she was unable to survive on that meager salary; so she came to the United States planning to work for four years, save money, and return home to start a business.

After the pollero and group left the two, María and her twenty-five-year-old nephew traveled alone in the desert for three days. They had no food. They ran out of water. She told how they ate ants and the pads and fruit of the prickly pear cactus. Her eyes reddened and began to water as she related the experience. She said the tears were not from recalling the pain, but the desperation. Her lips had been stained red from eating the cactus fruit, and she had gotten cactus spines in her mouth—glochids, those fine, little, hairlike spines that grow around the long sharp needles on the cactus pads and on the fruit. Along the way they came upon a small mesquite tree with many forked branches. There in the fork of the tree someone had left a prayer card with an image of the Virgin of Guadalupe and an *oración*, or prayer, written on the back of the card. María knew when she saw this that they would be rescued. She said she had felt the protective hand of the Virgin all along her journey.

Juan Miguel told of the journey through the desert with a group. One night as they stretched out under scrubby mesquite trees to sleep, he looked up and saw an image of the Virgin of Guadalupe outlined in the bark on a small tree trunk. He took this as a sign that they would have a successful journey.

Juan Miguel and his wife, Concha, were returning from a short stay in Mexico. They had lived in Florida for several years and had been home to visit family in Guanajuato. He said that in Florida he worked pouring concrete and showed me with circular hand motions how he smoothed out the cement. An affable young man, his wide grin framed teeth outlined in silver. Both muscular arms had tattoos, which he wore like showy costume jewelry. I wondered if this reflected his Florida life. Not many of the migrants coming through the desert have tattoos. High on his right arm was a red heart with cherubs on either side holding a banner and the name "Concepción" written across it. On his forearm below was an eagle, and around his left wrist was tattooed a dark blue chain, like a bracelet. On his left upper arm you could see part of an image of the Virgin. Her face wasn't visible, but sneaking out from below his sleeve was the Virgin's pink dress and green robe and the cherubic angel below her. Red and gold rays of light formed a scalloped border around the portion of her image that I could see.

A cousin and three brothers traveled with Concha and Juan Miguel. Together they had crossed the border and headed north until they reached a secondary road where they met their transport contact. The vehicle with a driver and six passengers was speeding along the extremely curvy Arivaca Road. The driver cut the steering wheel sharply as they rounded a curve, and the car plunged over the shoulder into a ravine. All occupants of the vehicle were taken to the hospital. Juan Miguel, his cousin, and one of the brothers were released that day. Concha, who is diabetic, was kept in the hospital for two days longer. She said that when the car plunged over the precipice, at the point of impact there was an aura of white light surrounding them, and the Virgin was there saying that everything would be all right.

Two brothers remained in the hospital several days. One had a ruptured spleen from the accident and it had to be removed. As he awoke from the haze of anesthesia after the operation, he had a vision of the Virgin. She told him to go home, back to Mexico. He would not be able to work for a while because of his surgery. He and his brothers decided to return home. Back to Guanajuato.

As he was being discharged, one brother took from around his neck an amulet bearing the image of the Virgin. He gave it to the nurse, Sarah, and asked for her prayers for him, his brothers, and the families to whom they were returning.

Story Two

~ KATHRYN

We crossed the border from Sonoyta, Sonora, Mexico, onto American soil. A friend and I were driving along the dark Arizona highway at midnight when suddenly lights blinded us. Big stadium lights so bright we had to lower the windshield visors. It was a Border Patrol checkpoint, rigid-faced uniformed men with guns telling us to stop.

It took me back to Germany years ago. Late one night, I climbed on a platform high above the guard station, Checkpoint Charlie, in Berlin, days before the wall fell. I could look over to the other side of the Berlin Wall. Searing white lights, soldiers, guns. A no-man's-land full of buried land mines. On this Arizona highway, I had to remind myself that this was my country; I was not in foreign occupied territory.

The Border Patrol lights pooled around saguaros and creosote bushes. In the light, nothing moved but agents and the U.S. vehicles they were searching. At the edge of the circle of light was an unclaimed and absolute darkness.

A few miles after leaving the checkpoint, we drove off the road and got out of the car to take a break. We leaned against the car in a desert full of rumors and shadows. Not far away, in complete silence, we saw a flashlight flicker on and off. A few minutes later and a few yards farther, again light flickered.

We drove deeper into the night along the Tohono O'odham Indian Nation. We passed two trucks sitting side by side in a wash, headlights off, only the wink of a cigarette lighter.

A half hour later, the shapes of two men in black with backpacks trudged along the highway, ducking into shadow as our headlights lit up their eyes.

On we drove into the darkness toward Tucson.

Story Three

Do you have other children?" I asked Alicia. She said no, then nothing else. She remained silent, looking straight ahead, eyes fixed on the car in front of us. She had been discharged from the hospital two days before, leaving behind the remains of her baby that had been born dead less than a week after she began her trek through the desert. We were sitting at a stoplight, and I glanced sideways at her. Wavy black hair fell down her back and reached below her waist. She was pretty in a scrubbed-clean way, pretty in a sad way. At first she appeared detached, but looking closer, I could tell it was sadness. There was no light in her eyes.

We were on our way to the Mexican consulate. They would cover the cost for cremation of the infant and would help her get papers so she could take the ashes back to Mexico. The *consulado* would make arrangements for transfer of the baby's body from the hospital to the funeral home, the final destination for far too many border crossers.

At home in Michoacán she had helped support her mother, sisters, and an eight-month-old nephew. Her fifteen- and sixteen-year-old sisters were still in high school and did not work. The family wanted them to graduate since Alicia had not had the opportunity to advance past primary school. She had worked in a Coca-Cola plant making sixty-five dollars a week for seven years. It was hard work but steady. Sometimes she worked from six in the morning until ten at night, working overtime to make extra money. But then the plant closed, and she was only able to get temporary work. Her grandfather was diagnosed with cancer, accumulated a lot of medical bills, and treatment was very expensive. Alicia's severance pay from the Coca-Cola plant was used to pay for his care. Her mother made only forty dollars a week at a domestic cleaning job. There was not enough money to support the family, so twenty-eight-year-old Alicia headed north to earn more money. She planned to send most of her earnings home to help with living expenses for the family and school expenses for her sisters. Six months pregnant, with the promise of a job picking fruit in Oregon, she set out on her journey.

As we rode to the consulate I attempted a few words of conversation. This was the first time I had met her. In some way I wanted to comfort her, ease the pain of loss of her child. But she seemed reluctant to talk, so I drove in silence.

Later I learned that the father of her baby, a man she had been with for two years, was not upset when she phoned him that the baby was born dead. She said he wasn't even sad when she left to come *al otro lado*. Alicia had been hurt by his lack of caring. She had even found out that he was "a type of man who would go out and look for other women."

Alicia and I sat in the office of the *consulado*. There was constant activity and people moving back and forth between the rooms, carrying messages to various officials. Amid all the bustling Alicia looked out of place, a disconnected look in her eyes. At a desk in the corner a pretty young woman with dark hair and perfectly arched eyebrows helped Alicia. She was kind and sympathetic, and Alicia responded to her. She was a representative of the consulate and went to the area hospitals to help Mexican nationals who had been hospitalized. On the wall behind her desk was a large board with posted information regarding several patients in various hospitals. The board, marked off in quadrants, was like a scoreboard where the score increases or decreases from one panel to the next, top to bottom, left to right. The seriousness of the medical condition worsened from one quadrant to the next, while the likelihood of survival declined.

In the top left quadrant was Imelda. Her diagnosis: dehydration.

In the bottom left quadrant was José Nicolás Alvarez, born 1985, admitted to the hospital with a fractured leg that required surgery.

In the top right quadrant was Candelaría Ortega Mendoza, a thirty-year-old female. Diagnosis: dehydration. She required dialysis every day because of renal failure secondary to rhabdomyolysis. The latter was not written on the board, but that is the most likely cause of renal failure in this circumstance—walking for days in the desert in blistering heat, with very little rest, becoming severely dehydrated. Rhabdomyolysis is a condition where the muscle cells begin to break down and the protein from the muscle cells gets into the bloodstream and circulates through the body. In the filtration job the kidneys perform, this muscle protein becomes trapped in the microscopic tubules of the kidneys and causes the kidneys to shut down.

In the same quadrant with Candelaría's information was written in brackets *[Samaritans will help with her]*. I was taken aback. I read it again. Samaritans will help with her? How could we help? The help of Samaritans lies in trying to prevent kidney failure, prevent heat illnesses, prevent dehydration that results in renal shutdown. We take water to the desert crossers before they need to go to the hospital. We bandage blistered feet, splint sprained ankles and knees, and rehydrate those who have been vomiting from drinking cattle-tank water. We encourage those who cannot keep up with their group to go back. We advise them to return home rather than risk a journey with Santa Muerte, Saint Death. The patient was on dialysis. What could Samaritans do?

I looked back to the dry-erase board. In the bottom right quadrant of the board was the last patient, Francisco Portes de la Peña. Date of birth: April 19, 1964. Diagnosis: fractured hip and cerebral lesions. Then below written ominously: *unconscious—on respirator.*

Alicia was still talking with the consular representative, but the hospitalized patients crowded my consciousness. I pictured them in another setting, all in the same hospital room, lying in a ward of four patients. On the other side of that thin, white curtain lay Candelaría. On the opposite side of the room would be José across from Imelda. Next to him, across from Candelaría, was Francisco. There are few hospitals that have patient wards arranged like that today. But in the late 1960s, when I was an intern and medical resident, many hospital wards had beds lined up on each side of the room across from each other.

Alicia was explaining to the representative the progression of events that had resulted in her hospitalization. When she began her journey, six months pregnant by her estimate, she felt movement of her baby. Every day she felt it kick. But several days of walking in the scorching desert sun took its toll: dehydration with symptoms of dizziness, nausea, and weakness. One day she felt the kicking and the next day no movement at all. Then she began to feel sick. She became very alarmed when her water broke. At this point she very demonstrably pantomimed the gush of amniotic fluid from between her legs. Two women who were traveling with her group of twenty stayed with her when she was abandoned by the coyote and rest of the group. The three of them went to the highway and flagged down help and were finally picked up by *la migra*. Alicia was taken to the hospital, and her friends were deported to Mexico immediately.

In the cool air-conditioning of the office the forms were completed. Alicia signed an affidavit as to her identity, since she had lost all of her identification papers in the desert. They assured her they would call when the ashes could be picked up, probably in two or three days.

After we left the consulate, Alicia's mood didn't change much. It was somewhere between stoic and pensive; maybe she had just withdrawn to another place, somewhere more comforting.

Fifteen days later I was back again in the office of the consulado. I had returned to get the ashes of baby boy Ortiz. Alicia had already left Tucson, but we promised to mail the ashes so her baby could be buried in Mexico. As I waited on the paperwork, I found myself once more sitting in front of the corner desk looking again at the board on the wall. It was empty. There were a few black smudges where part of a name wasn't completely erased. I wondered if the empty board meant there were no Mexican nationals in the hospitals at that time. What happened to the four who were on this board two weeks ago?

The patient on the respirator probably had died. The two who were in the first tier probably had been discharged. What about the woman on dialysis? Maybe she recovered. Possibly she was sent back home to Mexico. If so, I hoped that she lived in a city large enough to get good medical care.

Instead of a square divided into quadrants, the wall I was looking at now was divided into four equal squares side by side. To the left of the blank dry-erase board was a large, square picture frame holding a portrait of Benito Juárez, less Indian-appearing than most pictures of him. To the left of Juárez was a poster showing Mayan ruins. Initially it looked like a travel poster, but across the top in a diagonal banner was written the command in Spanish, ¡Vote! The last square was a black-and-white poster with three crosses and a cemetery with gravestones. Across the picture of the crosses was written in Spanish, "¡No expongas a los tuyos! ¡No dejes tu vida en el desierto!" (Do not put yourself at risk! Do not die in the desert!)

An official came to the door and beckoned me inside his office. I was handed the ashes in a little black box with a file folder label taped on it. José Ortiz Mendoza, the label said. I took it home to wait for the proper paperwork from the consulate before mailing the small container. I placed it on a ledge over the kiva fireplace in my living room, right beside the urn that is for my own ashes.

Story Four

~ KATHRYN

His skin was marble smooth. A fine coat of dust covered his chest; tiny pebbles stuck to the coffee-colored skin where his back lay flat against the dirt. Levi's hung loose around the long outstretched legs. His face was turned to the sky, a carpet of black eyelashes holding down the eyelids. The lips were slightly parted. Although the sun stabbed his body like a thousand ice picks, there was no moisture on his skin.

I wondered how he looked with his eyes open. I wondered how he looked when he laughed. I wondered what his voice sounded like when he sang. I wondered if he danced. I wondered who loved him.

But surely those were illegal thoughts. If the eleven Border Patrol agents standing around us could read my mind, I might have been arrested. In a culture that says, "We've apprehended nine bodies," there is little room for passion. Consorting with an "alien" is fodder for arrest. Does wondering about one make me culpable? Although, the truth of the matter is, they didn't see us. Even the six feet two Rock Hudson look-alike, holding up the plastic IV bag that dripped fluids into the man lying by my side, forgot we were there. He was telling his buddy how yesterday they had arrested a migrant for throwing rocks. We were not important.

We had been driving south on Route 286, headed for the trails off Elkhorn Road, when we came upon two Border Patrol vehicles. Three agents had five men in custody, all sitting in the dirt. As per Border Patrol requirement, we asked permission of the agent in charge if we could give water to the migrants. Agent Ramirez said sure, he was already out of water. It was a hot June day, 100 degrees at 9:30 a.m. We were working under a killer sun. Ramirez didn't object when Susan, our nurse, asked to check the men's vital signs. Everyone was dehydrated and had muscle cramps.

When she got to the last man, he was inert, sitting slumped over, arms folded across his knees. She asked his name. Aurelio, he whispered. She said to me, "This guy doesn't look good." Susan didn't speak Spanish and asked if I would find out if he had vomited or had diarrhea. He never spoke, kept his eyes shut, and shook his head. He nodded when asked if he was nauseated. She took his blood pressure. It was low, 80/40. We had him lie down. She felt for his pulse and took his blood pressure again. It was still low, only 90/40. She couldn't feel his pulse at the wrist, so listened to his chest with the stethoscope. She said he needed an IV.

I asked Ramirez if we could take him to St. Mary's Hospital, that we could be there in forty minutes. He said, "No, they're in custody." Shortly, another Border Patrol vehicle stopped, and three agents walked over to talk with Ramirez. He wanted them to take Aurelio to the hospital. They said he was just dehydrated, didn't look bad enough. Ramirez and another agent argued. Ramirez called Border Patrol Search, Trauma, and Rescue. BORSTAR was organized to help agents who had been injured in the field but is now called for emergencies with migrants. It was 10:00 a.m.

Twenty minutes later, three BORSTAR agents drove up, not in the blaze of action that their fire-engine-red shirts might imply. They casually got out of the van. The female agent greeted the other agents, filled out charts, checked Aurelio's vital signs, and said, "Start an IV."

There were now nine agents at the scene. They stood in several groups, talking. The four other migrants were quiet, still sitting on the ground. The sun had moved, and now a mesquite tree offered them a little shade.

When the IV was finished, the tall, dark-haired agent turned his back to us and dropped his arm down, holding the IV bag like a purse. I sat on the ground by Aurelio.

"Where were they throwing the rocks?" asked the one agent.

"Near Naco, from this side of the fence," said the other.

"How many?"

"Two."

"Who was in charge?"

"Smith and Moreno were both there."

Aurelio wasn't moving; so to keep him alert I asked him where he was from.

Instead of answering, he asked, "Are they the *migra*?"

"Yes."

"What are they going to do with me?"

"Take you to detention."

"I'm scared."

"They won't hurt you."

The tall blond agent turned and stepped toward us. Like all the other agents standing around, he wore a uniform, vest, and heavy boots. On his belt he carried a pistol, pepper spray, handcuffs, a folding knife, and a radio.

"What's he saying?" the agent asked.

I looked up at him. "He's afraid."

"Of what?"

"You guys."

"Why? Does he have something to hide?"

Looking up at this menacing image, I laughed and shook my head. "No, he's half-conscious and he's scared."

The agent turned and kept talking to his friend.

For a long time, Aurelio just lay there. He didn't speak anymore. I felt that something wasn't right. He didn't seem natural. He didn't move at all, not even his fingers or eyes. It looked like he wasn't breathing. His chest barely rose and fell.

"Hey, I think something is wrong," I said.

The agents quit talking and came over to us. They assessed Aurelio again and started a second IV. Ramirez walked over to ask what was going on. The BORSTAR lady explained they had to give a second IV. He said, "We're not doing much good here. Let's call a helicopter." He returned to his vehicle to call. It was 10:30 a.m.

Two more agents arrived in a jeep, slapped each other on the back, and chatted with the others. Now there were eleven agents and five Border Patrol vehicles. Some men were friendly with each other. It wasn't clear who was in charge. It seemed that several wanted to be. A few agents stood by their trucks on the road. Others were near the four migrants. The BORSTAR agents talked near Aurelio. The sun moved across the sky, heat increased. The men's uniforms had damp spots under the arms and down the back.

The agent holding the IV bag turned to his friend. "Did you see the D'backs last night?" he asked.

"Yeah, that was some game, but the Padres might beat 'em."

"I don't know—their bats are pretty strong. Craig Counsell is hitting over 400."

"Yeah, I think San Diego can take 'em."

I watched Aurelio. He wasn't moving.

Kathryn Ferguson and visiting Rabbi talk with migrants in the desert.

Susan walked over and said, "Hey, guys, can we at least move him to the shade?" He had baked in the sun almost two hours.

"Were you at the game?" the agent asked as they lifted Aurelio to the sparse shade of a mesquite tree.

"Naw, saw it in the office with Connors and Robinson."

As they talked baseball, twenty feet away, Ramirez asked where was their helicopter. An agent in the truck said there was a problem.

"What problem?" barked Ramirez.

"They can't seem to locate our position."

"What the hell's wrong with them?"

"I really don't know, sir."

"Well, cancel the damn thing. We've waited forty-five minutes already. Call the paramedics in Three Points. Tell them to get out here now."

It was 11:15. The Border Patrol helicopter still hadn't arrived. It had been lost for almost an hour. We were on Route 286, a paved secondary highway connecting a small community called Three Points directly to the town of Sasabe at the border. The only other main north–south artery within a hundred miles was Interstate 19. On a map, this road is a bold straight line. Anyone can see it.

I sat near him again. It was hot. Sweat poured down my face. Aurelio was fading. His head rolled to the side. His mouth remained loose and slightly open. In the middle of all these people, no one was looking at him. No one really cared, yet we had to ask permission for every move we made. Their rule is ask. And they often say no. We are required to ask permission to give water. We ask to give food. We ask to give socks. We ask to take vital signs. We ask permission to move a man from sun to shade. We ask to carry a semiconscious man to a hospital. We ask for a moment of light under a shadow of control cast by the deus ex machina of world order. To give water is not a grand gesture. What has happened that we have to beg permission to offer water to a thirsty man? This is not the way of the desert. We are out of whack.

At 11:30 a.m., two hours since we had first stopped, Three Points paramedics arrived. They moved quickly, put Aurelio in the emergency vehicle. It would be yet another forty minutes' travel time to the hospital. At this point, there were eleven Border Patrol agents, two paramedics, and four Samaritans—all gathered to deal with five sick, unarmed men. Three senior agents were shouting orders at the others. There were conflicts of opinions. Finally, as the ambulance drove away to St. Mary's Hospital in Tucson, Agent Ramirez said, "We could have had that guy to the hospital and back twice by now."

In the evening, we called St. Mary's to see if Aurelio had lived. They had no record of him. We called all the hospitals in Tucson. No one had heard of him. It was the same answer for the hospital in Sells, on the Tohono O'odham Nation, the hospital nearest Three Points. We could find out nothing more about Aurelio. It was as if it had never happened.

Group waits in wash for pickup by their coyote.

Story Five

We sit inside the church the night before a patrol. There are fifty-plus of us. We were told it was important to be there, because some valuable information was going to be shared. Our General in this battle is passionate about the cause and must be, absolutely, for we are completely outnumbered in every way imaginable, except in faith. In this our little army is strong. Those whose beliefs are worn as a badge in the field are assembled, and others who support are there in spirit. It is a ragtag little group but feisty and, I sense, battle-hardened. No one will back down, no one will cower in fear; they will stand tall in support of the faith of their actions.

The General is here tonight to give us warning. Our foe is getting stronger, feeding on fear and ignorance. It grows larger and more deadly. It has become so dangerous that we must be very conscious of our actions, more so than ever, and be mindful of the consequences lest we harm ourselves or the cause. Although the news is sobering, I sense no foreboding or despair, only resolve to continue the good fight with a new sense of respect for our adversary and continuing admiration for all those who stand up for what can be described as kindness and decency to fellow travelers in this part of the world. I bike home into the darkness; tomorrow I will do what I can.

We are deeply into the first week of February, and I cannot remember a winter as warm and dry. The truck is loaded when I arrive, and we are out into the early morning with lovely Venus burning a hole in the eastern sky and no moon.

The pink rays of morning are forming to the east when we come across the two travelers. I slow the truck to twenty-five as we pass, and a man looks at us in confusion and hopefulness. His companion, a woman, looks a bit disheveled and glances at our truck as well. They both look tired and sleepy.

I pull off the shoulder of the road to turn around as the cavalry arrives from the west. Two Border Patrol squad cars burning high octane spot us and the two travelers at the same moment. They brake hard and pull off the road in a cloud of dust to start this day's body count. I cannot help but say, "Damn. We're too late."

I consult with my two compadres, and we decide to go across the road and offer food and water. The couple looks quite haggard, and the woman has grass matted into her jet-black hair from where she rested her head last. The man looks at our truck for some reassurance, and the red insignia on the door registers somewhere in his weary mind. Perhaps he thinks we will intervene with the *migra* and take them to a place where they can take a shower, put on some clean clothes, and eat some warm food. Maybe they have made it? The Samaritan approaches, and the Border Patrol agents give him permission to offer food. I stay in the truck. I cannot look at the couple's faces; I do not want to look. They accept the baggies filled with granola bars and Vienna sausage and crackers, and we melt back onto the highway as the sun spills out onto the Baboquivari Mountains.

Heading south, we go down a ranch road a way and then spot a well-worn trail and walk north. The land is bare except for cactus, creosote, and the occasional stand of mesquite and palo verde. It feels hot already. We see deer. We see a calf whose left rear leg is injured; she can't put weight on it. She hobbles away from us, running ahead a hundred feet and then stopping, running again and then stopping, never thinking until we drop off into a small arroyo to go sideways. We continue along, singing out our song in Spanish: "Hello, we are friends. We have water, food, and medical help. We are friends from a church, Samaritans." We come across a steer whose entire face is filled with the pincushion of the cholla cactus. He looks hideous and pissed off. We turn around then and go back to the truck.

Farther south, we are again heading west on a dirt road. This land has not been grazed, and there is abundant dry grass. We drive until we hit the gate where a cowboy hauling a horse trailer is coming out. He motions for us to stop. He wants to talk. He saunters over to our rig, the forty-five holstered, big bushy mustache, chaps, and a denim shirt.

"Are you the people puttin' water out on the land?"

"No, we don't do that."

"What do you do?"

"We drive around looking for migrants in need of medical attention, or food and water, and then we help them."

"Oh? Well, the last thing I want to find out here is a dead person. They're drinking out of my cattle tanks. That water'll make 'em sick."

"We know."

"Well, can you get those people to put water out here?"

"Sure, we can tell them, but who do they contact to get permission? Can we get your phone number?"

"You don't need my permission. It's public land. The Border Patrol comes out here sometimes, but they're drinking out of them tanks and I just don't want to find somebody dead."

"We'll tell them, and thank you. You need any medical attention? We have a nurse on board."

"I'm fine, thank you."

I'm not sure if he thought that was funny or not. His poker face was hard to read. You're never sure where you will run into a bit of grace, but I'm always thankful when it comes my way.

We continue toward the border, and at a crossroads three Border Patrol cars have just pulled over a mid-eighties Ford pickup with Sonora plates. As we approach, two agents have automatic weapons trained on the cab. We approach very slowly. The driver is roughly removed from the truck and shoved to the side of the road. We drive past, and the agents see we are on the scene. We stop next to a crew of men burying fiber-optic cable. I ask them what is going on. "Is it drugs?" I ask. "Probably," the foreman says. The agent in charge of the scene is yelling at someone in the cab to get out of the truck. A woman and child exit. My Samaritan partners at this point get water and food packets out and begin to walk across the road to offer them. The agent in charge goes ballistic and tells them, "Get back across the road and do not move until we have secured the bodies!"

The two Samaritans retreat. The foreman of the work crew asks me to move our truck because a big cement truck is coming and our vehicle is in the way. I move the truck across the road and miss the unveiling of the false bottom in the pickup where twelve people are lying down. Four of them are children. They are herded under a mesquite tree. After the agents fill out some paperwork, the one in charge bellows out, "Okay, you can offer them food now." The Samaritans carry the big plastic container full of food packets over to the migrants.

I watch from the other side of the road. I can't get close to these people at this moment. I need some detachment. Like the cowboy says, "I just don't want to find somebody dead."

Story Six

~ KATHRYN

B *lood was up to his anklebones. His Wellington boots were orchid red. The humid room smelled of death, and he wasn't used to the stench. As bile came up from his throat to his mouth, he gagged. He glanced around the kill floor to see if anyone noticed. Next to him, his compadre with the missing fingers made a hard slice from throat to belly. Down the line, another man ripped back a hide. Another man tied off the intestines. And another shaved flesh from the head until it was as transcendental as Longhorn skulls floating on the walls of Texas restaurants. Can I get used to this, he wondered? A man gets accustomed to anything, he reminded himself.*

As I was settling into the plush emerald velvet seat, my friend pointed out a man standing by the entrance to the theater. He wore a dark, square-shouldered leather jacket with red piping that edged the collar and curled around the front pockets. He had on a black silk shirt, dark pants, and gleaming pointed-toed cowboy boots. He was average height with thinning dark hair, and he laughed easily with the man standing next to him. My friend said, "See that good-looking guy? That's my cousin, Dagoberto García."

As the lights dimmed, the last of the five hundred patrons moved to their seats, filling the theater to capacity. It was amphitheater style with the rows in a semicircle, back row highest, descending to front-row seats at stage level. Dago sat across from us.

The Teatro de los Héroes in Chihuahua City was filled with patrons, politicians, and artists who came to see the play *La Mujer que Cayó del Cielo* (The Woman Who Fell from the Sky) in honor of its author, Victor Hugo Rascón Banda, the beloved Mexican playwright. He was to be honored by the governor after the play.

House lights blackened as stage lights rose. The stage was mostly dark. A spotlight lit an abstract window made of prison bars suspended in air. Below the window, behind bars of a jail cell, a frightened woman in a long flowered dress crouched in shadow. Another spotlight focused on two policemen playing cards, talking. One officer asked where they found her. The other explained she was eating from a refrigerator in a private home. The first one said where did she come from? That's the big mystery—she doesn't speak English, said the other. Both men agreed that since she didn't speak English and her behavior was crazy, they should lock her up.

The play was about Rita, who walked 1,500 miles from Mexico's Barranca del Cobre to Kansas. She was arrested and placed in a Kansas mental hospital for ten years because her unrecognized native language was thought to be the "guttural noises" of a mentally ill person. She was a Tarahumara Indian. Although she spoke no English and couldn't communicate, an American judge declared her mentally ill and placed her in a psychiatric hospital. It was a riveting, true story about a journey that haunts the landscape between three cultures.

In the dark, I looked across the row at Dago. He was absorbed in the drama, never taking his eyes from the stage.

When the play and speeches were over, we moved to the lobby for champagne and hors d'oeuvres, hundreds of people laughing gaily for the media's flashing camera lights, or intensely arguing over the treatment of Rita and others who migrate to the United States.

My friend introduced me to her cousin. He was gracious, easy to talk to, even with my choppy Spanish. I apologized for not speaking fluently. Careful, he said leaning close, they might lock you in a mental hospital for not speaking the language. We were momentarily interrupted by a woman next to us talking in a loud voice. She was dressed in a long purple chiffon gown, her black hair wrapped high on her head, diamonds dangling from her ears. We looked around.

"See," Dago whispered, "we are surrounded by the elite of Chihuahua."

"Looks like politicians over there," I said.

"You can spot them a kilometer away," he laughed.

The men were in tuxedos. The women next to them were a dazzling rainbow of silk, jewels, and scarlet lip gloss.

"Looks like they are from Barrio Volvo," I said.

"More like Barrio Mercedes," he added. "Speaking of politicians, what's the difference between our Mexican government and your President Bush's government?"

"I don't know, what?"

"Our government is run by a crook surrounded with idiots. Yours is run by an idiot surrounded by . . ."

I laughed. "You're right."

Munching on olives stuffed with tiny chiles, I asked, "What did you think of the play?"

"Great. Well written. Sad. Unfair," he said. "But I just can't imagine why anyone would choose to take such a chance with her life and cross the Chihuahuan Desert. You could die out there. I guess you would have to be pretty desperate to do that."

Two years later, Dago would cross the desert.

When I met Dago, he was a Muppie, a Mexican yuppie. He had a great job, two houses, a beautiful wife, and two beautiful adoring daughters. There was a lot of laughter in his life. He worked hard for Levi Strauss's Mexico division as an executive. He flew from city to city, overseeing textile plants, making sure company finances were in order, and because he was a generous man, making sure employees were treated well. He traveled all over Mexico.

His wife, Elena, was manager of a computer equipment company. She felt blessed to have a smart, handsome, energetic husband and two great girls. She sometimes worried about her husband, that he worked too hard, didn't relax enough. She liked having a good job. Often, after working sixty hours during the week, she would make reservations at a resort. She and Dago would take Friday, Saturday, and Sunday and go to the brilliant white beaches of Acapulco. She knew they deserved it. And she really liked to look beautiful for her husband. She adored dressing up for him in her designer clothes.

One balmy April day, Dago was called into the boss's office. "There's a rumor," his boss said, "that they're going to close."

"Who?" asked Dago.

"Levi Strauss," the boss said.

"Us?"

"Yes, us."

"How can that be? This is a huge U.S. company."

"It's a huge international company," said his boss. "Even if we are doing a good job, doesn't mean much. At the meeting yesterday, we were told that in order for Levi Strauss to stay competitive, they might have to shut us down."

"But we have no problems here; we meet all the requirements," Dago protested.

"Don't forget, 'we' have nothing to do with it," his boss replied.

"It's a U.S. company. We're totally dependent on them."

"I thought NAFTA was supposed to help," said Dago.

"You're smarter than that," said his boss. "Look, here's how it is. As long as we function like a maquiladora, we can't produce enough garments . . . we don't pull in enough money. Since NAFTA started, our outlet just isn't big enough. Levi Strauss is moving the maquilas to Central America or Asia. They can get cheaper labor."

"Mexican labor is too expensive for the U.S.? What a joke."

"The only way we can compete is if we make the whole package. They said they can only work with Mexican companies that do it all—design, product development, marketing, retail—not just manufacturing. It's like the companies in Torreón. They're big and they're changing over to a full package production. We're a small business; we're going to go under."

"I can't believe this is happening."

His boss said that Americans say Mexican business is like a dangerous serpent, but he thought of American businessmen as one-eyed ogres who see only the dollar sign and bite off the head of the serpent for lunch. Dago didn't laugh.

Soon after Dago spoke with his boss, Levi Strauss closed sixty-eight textile plants in Mexico, including his. Dago tried to get jobs in the few remaining companies but couldn't. He interviewed, waited, interviewed, waited.

His wife worked longer hours to make more money to pay the bills. It was hard to work so much and take care of the kids. She told Dago that since he wasn't working, he needed to help more with the girls and the housekeeping. He wasn't happy about it, but he did. His sister-in-law moved in to help, another mouth to feed. They just needed a little more time. They would make it.

After a year, Dago got another job managing a company that made automobile parts. The money wasn't as good and the hours were longer, but at least it was a job. They were able to make payments on their loans for the two houses, repair their car. It was better, but Elena was still worried about money. They couldn't cover all the expenses every month, worked longer hours, and never went to Acapulco. She didn't like the way Dago sat around after work. He used to be more energetic, but now he came home and just sat. She decided he should get an additional job to make ends meet. They had never-ending discussions about that.

One evening, Dago didn't arrive home. Elena thought maybe he got another job. Her parents came over. Her mom and daughters made dinner. They finished dinner. Dago still hadn't come home. They cleaned the kitchen, her parents left. Much later, Dago walked in the door without speaking. "What is it?" she asked. "This company's closing, too. I have one more week of work," he said.

For weeks, Dago looked for work, calling friends, acquaintances, anyone who might know of a job. After a while, he stopped looking. His wife thought him to be a very selfish man. Lazy. She began to get angry. They couldn't pay the bills. They couldn't afford the good food they were accustomed to eating. But most of all, she hadn't been able to buy clothes for a long time. She didn't really want to dress up for her husband anymore. She was embarrassed for her friends to see her in the same clothes all the time.

Elena told Dago that she didn't want him around the house. She said he should move into their other house. He looked for work again and could only find work that paid eight dollars a day. He didn't take those jobs. His family needed and deserved things that those jobs would not support. He was embarrassed. He loved his wife and daughters. He remembered how they used to laugh and travel. How could he have let his life fall apart like this? He didn't blame them for being angry with him.

A fear centered itself deep inside Dago. It crawled through his dreams, cluttered his daily thoughts. He feared he would end up like his cousin Esai and his family. They lived in Morelos near the border. They lived in an adobe house that was so small you had to close the front door to open the oven door.

Esai worked at a maquiladora. He earned fifty dollars per week standing all day at an assembly line screwing on the tops of flashlights. Since he had a quota, he couldn't leave his position on the line to go to the bathroom to urinate until his shift ended. In Chicago, a gardener earns Esai's weekly salary in half a day's work. In Morelos, thousands of jobs disappeared when American-run maquilas closed down in the middle of the night, taking products across the line and not paying workers. A few years ago, Esai earned four dollars per hour; now it was one dollar per hour.

Dago wondered if that could possibly happen to him. He promised himself that he would never let it get that bad.

The bank said it would call in their loan, so they sold their second house. His life came to an abrupt halt. Elena said she wanted a divorce. She would keep the girls, of course.

Two years after I spoke with Dago at the theater in Chihuahua, he crossed over. After a long journey, he arrived in a Nebraska town.

It had a population of two thousand, with two-story houses of white siding and wrap-around porches, and streets named Pine or Walnut laid in a grid. The town had two motels run by Pakistanis, and a Wal-Mart out on the highway. At the edge of town, there was a runway with an upside-down crop duster that had flipped during heavy prairie winds.

Dago rented an apartment and applied for work. No one would hire him—no papers, no job. Someone explained to him how the system worked. The next day he went to a private house, showed his birth certificate, driver's license, and other Mexican ID to a man sitting at a table cluttered with legal forms. Go home, have the money in cash, and we'll bring the papers you need on Thursday, he told Dago.

On Thursday, a man arrived at Dago's apartment with the papers. Dago paid $1,200 in exchange for the U.S. ID and work papers. On Friday, he went shopping at Wal-Mart. When he came home, the door to his apartment was open. He went in. Drawers and cabinets were open. His watch and the envelope with his ID papers were missing.

The fear came again. He panicked. He didn't know what to do. There was no one to talk to. He wouldn't be able to get a job. He had a little money left for food but wouldn't be able to pay the rent again. While looking for a job, he had met a man from Veracruz who was looking for work, too. He went to see him. The man told Dago that what happened to Dago happens to new immigrants all the time. The same man that Dago paid the $1,200 to came back to rob him.

Combing the streets, Dago tried to get work trimming hedges, sweeping sidewalks. He got a little work unloading a truck on a farm for a day. Everyone told him he should get a job in a slaughterhouse. Ugly work but great money, they said. He applied at three slaughterhouses, but with no identification, he couldn't get the job. One place said come back; they'd hire him when he figured out how to get papers.

He moved into an apartment with three other men. They all looked for work each day, but usually there was nothing. On the farms, they hired only men with work papers. The men in his apartment came and went. New faces every week. Strangers.

Dago wanted to hear his daughters' voices. It had been a month since they spoke. These feelings—it required a lot of energy to sort them out in his mind. He was tired. Plagued by the wizard of the unconscious, he rarely slept. Each night, just as he was about to sleep, his body jerked as he slid down through a narrow black tunnel with nothing to break his fall, his body ricocheting off sharp edges of blame.

He missed his two daughters. Although for weeks he wouldn't permit himself to finish the thought, he had a fear that the last time he saw them was the final time. The closeness between the three of them had been carried away by wolves that prowled the shadows of his journey.

During the day, for something to do, he walked the paved streets of the town and the dirt roads to the farms. When he hit the farmlands, he almost felt good until the dark being beneath his bones rose up to remind him that no one traveled with him.

His friend from Veracruz told him that he had heard about a blind woman in a nearby town who knew how to get work. It was said that she sometimes sat on a corner near the park. Dago felt better. He would look for this woman. Every few days, he walked six miles to the other town and went up and down the streets looking for her. He asked if anyone knew this blind woman. No one did. Finally, he saw her. She sat alone in a folding chair at the edge of the park. She was big and overflowed the chair. Her cane was on the ground beside her. He approached her but didn't know what to say. He felt shy, so he just stood near her. "¿Qué quiere?" she asked. What do you want? He said he was from Chihuahua and asked where she was from. "¿Qué quiere?" she said again. He said he had been in Nebraska for weeks and couldn't get a job. She said, "Why are you telling me?" He said his friend from Veracruz said she might help people find work. She said, "I don't know your friend from Veracruz and I don't know you. Go away."

Dago walked away. He drifted through the streets and alleys. He was hungry. As he passed a garbage bin, he saw a half-full bag of bread. Without thinking, he grabbed it. It was a first. He had never taken bread from a garbage can. He sat down by a tree. He was less than a street dog, he thought.

He got up and walked the streets, step by step, until the sun was about to go down. He saw a phone box with a telephone book. Are there any more like me here, he wondered. He looked under "G" for García, his name. There were nineteen Garcias in the surrounding small towns. He placed his phone card in the slot and called the first one.

"Hello, this is Dago García. Did you know my father Miguel Angel García from Chihuahua?" "No." Click. He called the next García.

"Hi, I'm Dagoberto Jose García Saenz. Do you know my father Miguel Angel?"

"No, never heard of him." Click.

On the fourteenth García, he dialed the number.

"Hi, this is Dagoberto Jose García Saenz from Chihuahua. Did you know my father Miguel Angel?"

"Who?" asked a woman's voice. He repeated. She said, "Yeah, my husband's cousin had an uncle with that name. You are Dago? What are you doing here?" He explained. She said come over for dinner. He accepted, hung up the phone, pressed his forehead against the phone box and cried.

He walked off the killing floor, dodging the skinned carcasses swinging from the revolving rack, and washed the blood from his boots. My present is this inferno and my past is dead, he thought. He stepped outside the slaughterhouse. He shrugged his shoulders. "Ni modo," he said out loud. Never mind.

Story Seven

Jesús recently sent me an e-mail in response to the photograph I sent of the completed labyrinth in our backyard. He says that he is doing well and his health is good. He is sorry that he was not able to complete the project he helped to begin. Jesús is happy to be back in Mexico and appreciative of all of the concern shown him and the help given to him while here. Most of all, he is grateful to live many migrants' dream: to return home and to work in his own country.

I first got to know Jesús when he came to help my husband do yard work. He was a soft-spoken, humble man. I learned that he was educated, had studied at the University in Chiapas, and had worked in agricultural jobs before coming to the United States.

Jesús was from the state of Campeche, on the Yucatán Peninsula, an area very rich in agriculture. As an employee of independent farmers, he worked hundreds of acres of greenhouses where tomatoes and other produce were grown. The enactment of the North American Free Trade Agreement (NAFTA) in 1994 affected all agricultural commerce in Mexico, but it had a tremendous impact in Campeche, where growing vegetables is a primary source of revenue and livelihood. With the passage of NAFTA, large international corporations moved in and took over agribusiness on the peninsula. They paid low wages to the workers and exported produce without having to pay tariffs. The independent tomato growers that Jesús worked for could not compete and closed their business, and Jesús lost his source of income. He said he could not even walk in the streets because creditors would hound him for money that he owed. He was unable to make payment because the clients to whom he sold vegetables were unable to pay him. Eventually he reached a compromise to settle with the owners of the produce business for half of what was due. Jesús was able to extricate himself from the debt but still did not have a job. He came to the United States with a plan to pick grapes for eight months. He wanted to earn enough money to go back to the Yucatán and start a community enterprise in horticulture. He had worked with women in his community who were unemployed and needed to work to support their children. He taught them how to grow flowers, his first love. He wanted to start a business and employ these women who have no other means of support.

At forty-seven, Jesús was older than most of the people crossing the border. But he was in good physical condition—a wiry, small man with no extra body fat. His heavy black eyebrows framed big, bulging eyes that smiled out at you from under the eyebrow canopy. His small frame belied his strength. He had a black belt in karate and prided himself on the fact that he ate a healthy diet and regularly exercised, but, as was not uncommon in middle-aged Latino men, he was diabetic. Diabetes causes a lot of problems in migrants crossing through the desert. Diabetes, cardiovascular disease, hypertension, pregnancy, seizures: these are all medical conditions that predispose to trouble in the desert. People in excellent health still get in trouble from dehydration and heat-related illnesses. For someone with an underlying medical problem the danger to their health is compounded. Migrants do not anticipate the extreme physical effort that will be demanded of them. Those who are diabetic are not prepared. Increased physical activity and exercise burn more sugar, so they run the risk of hypoglycemia if they are already on medications. They are unable to control the quality of their dietary intake, sometimes run out of their medicine, develop nausea, vomiting, and diarrhea, then become hyperglycemic. And, as was the case with Jesús, they are found in the desert in a coma due to diabetic ketoacidosis.

Jesús didn't remember who found him or how he got to the emergency room. It was probably by Border Patrol helicopter. But when he regained consciousness, he was hooked up to IVs and heart monitors, and there were tubes everywhere. He remained in the hospital for nine days. His diagnoses: diabetes mellitus, peptic ulcer, and hypertension. After being discharged, he continued his several medications for diabetes. His blood sugar remained high, fluctuating between 250 and 375 until he became more active. Once he began doing yard work and landscaping, his blood sugar dropped to near-normal levels, and his diabetic medications were decreased from two oral diabetic medications to one half-tablet daily.

In our backyard I introduced Jesús to my husband, who was getting ready to construct a labyrinth from the many rocks filling the earth behind our house. This was a big project, and my husband enjoyed the mathematical calculations of design as well as the exercise of moving the large stones and boulders. Now he needed more hands and a strong back to help clear the dry bursage and dead prickly pear and move some of the larger stones. When he saw Jesús, a small man, he was perplexed. He soon learned what a hard worker and how strong the small Mexican was. I tried to explain in my halting Spanish a little about the project.

"This area will need to be cleared of all the bursage," I told him, indicating the space Stan had marked off for the sixty-foot-diameter design. None of the ironwood trees would be affected, but a few scraggly mesquite trees would need to be dug up. One palo verde tree was within the design layout but would be incorporated into a pathway. Several large prickly pear clumps needed to be removed, and two barrel cacti had to be moved to another site. The challenging task was to transplant a saguaro about four feet high. Less than a hundred meters south of the labyrinth site was a craggy outcropping where there were thirty or more giant saguaro cacti of various age and character, with different arms and silhouettes. No two were exactly the same. These aged sentinels stood guard over the rocks, lizards, rabbits, and snakes.

"Once the plants are cleared, then the rocks can be put over in that area and used to outline the pathways," I said. Although he smiled and nodded, I was not sure he followed what I was trying to say in my broken Spanish. The rocks varied from the size of a basketball to the size of an orange. Smaller ones would be raked aside.

My husband does not speak Spanish, but he was good at communicating with gestures what needed to be done. He told Jesús that they were working on a labyrinth or maze. Since Jesús knew some English words as well, the work seemed to progress smoothly. However, after they had been working for two hours Stan came up to the house and asked, "How do you say labyrinth in Spanish? I'm afraid Jesús thinks we are going to plant corn."

He worked in our yard several days and worked for other people tending plants and landscaping. It brought him a lot of joy and satisfaction to work with the earth and grow things. When he departed Campeche, his destination had been California to work in the vineyards, where he hoped to earn enough money to return home before the end of the year. However, during his recuperation from the hospital stay, a young female volunteer suggested connecting him with Just Coffee, a business on the border that roasts, packages, and sells coffee grown in Chiapas under "fair trade" conditions. She was able to put him in touch with two of the directors of the business in Douglas, Arizona, and Agua Prieta, Sonora. They came to Tucson to interview Jesús and were enthusiastic at the prospect of having him work with them. They planned to orient him in the business; then he would go to Veracruz to expand the Just Coffee enterprise into that coastal state on the Gulf of Mexico.

So it was that Jesús made his way back to Mexico by a circuitous route. As soon as his blood sugar was regulated, Jesús headed south. I thought it very ironic that he was arrested returning to Mexico. Two members of the Christian Peacemaker Team who were spending the summer in southern Arizona were driving Jesús to Aqua Prieta, Mexico, where he would begin training with the Just Coffee business. Two miles north of the border the Arizona State Police stopped the trio headed south, and after checking identification documents the trooper called the Border Patrol. Jesús was taken into custody and detained over eleven hours without food, water, or medication before being taken back across the border to his home country.

Story Eight

~ KATHRYN

Twirling headsets in her hand, the woman in a gray suit walked over to two U.S. marshals sitting on a bench on the other side of the polished wood rail.

"I forgot to tell you what he said after that," she whispered.

"What?" the marshal asked.

"That this is America and you're not guilty until proven guilty."

"But he broke the law," the marshal laughed. "It's black and white."

Behind me, two lawyers entered the courtroom, patted each other on the back.

"I'm surprised to see you here, too."

"Yah, our office agreed to represent some of the defendants."

"How's your daughter?"

"A teenager—explanation enough?"

Two young women in green uniforms sat down on the bench across the row from me, exchanged chewing gum, laughed and talked.

The government lawyer in a brown box skirt and jacket, representing Border Patrol, dropped papers as she strode to her table on the other side of the railing. One of the two women chewing gum rushed to gather the papers for her.

Everyone seemed to know everyone. Smiles flew around the room along with greetings of good cheer. Papers rustled, people bustled. Wood gates swung back and forth, letting lawyers and bailiffs pass from the visitors' gallery to the courtroom proper.

On the other side of the room, it was complete silence. The only movement was the shaking thigh of a twenty-year-old dark-skinned man with Indian features, long black hair to midback tied away from his face.

The other seated fifty-one people either looked at the floor, or looked forward into a place the rest of us were not invited.

"All rise," a voice commanded.

The judge entered the court to a symphony of metal ringing against metal as the migrants rose, shifting shackled ankles in order to keep balance as they stood. All were handcuffed. The cuffs were attached to chains that were connected to the ankle shackles. Since all belts were taken by the Border Patrol, one man's loose jeans kept slipping down. He couldn't pull them up because his handcuffs were tautly connected to a chain around his waist.

In black flowing robes, the blonde judge walked to the bench. As she sat, we all took our seats. The stage was set. Operation Streamline, a Border Patrol policy, selects one hundred migrants a day to prosecute as criminals. From the hundreds detained daily, these are mysteriously chosen to be tried, convicted, and receive up to 180 days in prison as a misdemeanor for illegal entry into the United States. Then they are deported. If they return and are caught again, they can receive two to twenty years as a felony conviction.

"Good afternoon," said the judge.

There was a small pause as the migrants listened to the translation through their headsets. The translator told them to speak in unison. "Buenas tardes," the chorus called back to the judge.

"Stand and answer 'present' when your name is called," the judge said.

The translator called out "Number 341, Jose Luis Perez Moreno."

"Presente." The translator translated "present."

"Number 342, Mariaelena Ruiz Blanco."

"Presente."

After twenty more names, the judge called "Juan Alberto Martinez Ramos." A fifty-five-year-old man rose. Like all the migrants, he wore the same clothes he had been wearing in the desert four days earlier, the left shoulder torn open.

"Wheel," he said, "no Juan."

"What is he saying?" the judge asked.

"Mi nombre es Wheel," he quietly replied, pronouncing a soft "w" followed by a breath. Impatiently the judge demanded the translator explain.

"He said his name is Wheel."

"What is that?" she asked.

As his only remaining dignity lay in his name, the man wished to clarify it. "Wheel," he said again softly. The migrant's lawyer intervened.

He walked over to speak with the man. After a short discussion, the lawyer called out "Will. His name is Will Alberto Martinez Ramos." Mr. Martinez said "gracias" and sat down. The judge noted the correction and finished the roll call.

She said, "You have all been charged with illegally entering the United States. You have a right to a trial, which will be in thirty days. You have all waived the right to a trial. Do you understand?"

"Sí," the room replied.

"How do you plead?"

Culpable, culpable, culpable. "Guilty," fifty-two people said, one person at a time, the men looking straight ahead, women whispering it into the floor.

As the afternoon wore on, the federal public defenders stood before the judge with groups of defendants. They asked for time served for each person. All the defendants present in court that day had been held in a twenty-by-twenty-foot cell for four days and nights, fifty to sixty people in one small cell. Many had to sleep sitting up. One of those nights, a Border Patrol agent, angry with a migrant, took away all the blankets, so the migrants slept on cold concrete.

A lawyer explained to the judge that after the first eighteen hours in custody, each person received a meal of crackers after spending days in the desert.

The lawyers also explained that migrants' possessions were taken from them by Border Patrol. Agents told the migrants they had to sign a paper in order to receive their belongings. The paper is written in English. The paper states the opposite; if they sign it, they say they do not wish to receive what they brought with them and that their possessions can be destroyed after thirty days. Since they don't speak English, they don't understand what they signed. That means they will not get back their country's identification cards, their driver's licenses, money, medicines, clothes, or family photos.

Also, the lawyers explained to the judge that after migrants are picked up in the desert, they are locked in Homeland Security buses that are parked beside back roads in various desert locations where they may wait for hours until the bus is full before being taken to detention. If they tell the driver it is hot, the Homeland Security driver turns on the heater.

Lawyers also explained that in detention, if they ask for water, a bucket is set down and the Border Patrol whistles at the people to come drink from the bucket as if they are dogs. They cup their hands to get water.

One lawyer stood before the judge with a fifty-three-year-old man from Mexico. The Mexican explained that his wife had a heart attack and a blind son was unable to work. He had come here to earn money for the survival of his family. As he spoke, tears streamed down his face. He bent over and tried to wipe them away with the edge of his T-shirt but couldn't because his hands were chained at waist level.

The judge listened to all, then gave sentences ranging from 5 to 180 days in jail. She said she would look into the matters brought before her. We all rose as the judge left the courtroom. Then everyone began running about, singing out orders. Uniformed men grabbed fabric at the elbows, leading the men and women out the door, pulling them by their shirtsleeves. The symphony of chains began again.

At the end of court, all migrants were led out in front of us to a small holding cell. Some were embarrassed and wouldn't look at us. Some had tears in their eyes; some stared.

According to the lawyers, nothing has changed about the twenty-by-twenty cells, nothing has changed about heaters on the bus, and nothing has changed about food and water.

The show begins at 1:00 p.m. every afternoon. Open to the public.

Story Nine

~ TED

Have you ever looked into the eyes of your child, or your wife or husband or lover, and seen a look of panic, a sense they are stepping off into a zone they will or will not return from without some bloodletting? Ever seen it in a complete stranger? Ever felt that way yourself? Good.

I read in the local paper today that we've had one day of measurable rain in the last 119 days, and that was only 0.01 of an inch on December 12. We are approaching four months without rain. A part of me wants to see what would happen if we went a year without any. This is what happens in the desert. It stays dry for a long time. The wind whips up a fine dust that coats everything so the cactus and the trees and shrubs take on the same color as the dirt eventually. So do the people who wander about the landscape. Plants begin to shut down, conserving whatever bit of moisture they have stored up, and tiny leaves drop in droves. The trees look dead, though they are just dormant, waiting for the rains that do not come. The cholla drop their spiny pods, beavertail begin to shrivel, the saguaros lose half their circumference, and everything waits for the drought to end.

Very patiently we wait. Strange splits in the fingers and lips ooze a mixture of plasma and blood. It's impossible to keep the dust off your car, your shelves, your desk, your cabinets, your bed, and your life.

We headed out at 6:20 in the morning, a young man with my level of experience—or better, really—and me. A waning moon greeted us as we headed out onto a ranch road. Having heard on our trusty scanner that two migrants are on this road, we start down it and see the Border Patrol heading out onto the highway. He must have picked them up. We cruise for a while. We see a rancher taking the kids to the bus stop for school. Nothing else. We turn around and head back toward the pavement when we see him. His name is Alfonso. He is from Veracruz, Mexico. He has built a small fire by the road.

We talk to him. He wants a ride to Phoenix. He is desperate. My young friend tells him that we can't do it. He is okay, medically speaking. No aches or pains, and his feet are fine. We offer food and water. The group has left him. He had been sleeping and woke up and they were gone. He refuses the water and food. It's frustrating. You look in his eyes and see. You see he feels trapped like a rat. He is way deep into this shitty situation without the option to bail, except to walk back to Mexico, which he claims he will do. Don't call *la migra*, he says. He prefers to wait by the road, and maybe the Good Samaritans will pick him up and take him to a safe place and he can live happily ever after. But the other Samaritans are on the scene now.

He asks for a couple of dollars. He thinks they're worth a thousand pesos apiece. We let him know that a dollar is worth ten pesos. Eventually he accepts our food and water and melts back into the bush.

On the way back to the highway we hear dispatch ask for a unit to check on a reported campfire on this road. An agent says that he already picked one guy up, but he'll check it out, since he had not seen a fire when he was down the road before. We see him ten minutes later, heading in. We figure the rancher called it in, since there has been nobody else on the road. My young fellow traveler remarks that Alfonso will never trust Samaritans again.

We travel down another dirt road and hike north on a trail in an area known to contain sensors that go off when people walk near them. They are reported over the scanner as "Sector such and such" followed by some other numbers and then number of "hits," meaning the number of people who have crossed over the sensor at that given location. The Border Patrol has many of these sensors placed all over the desert—or so we figure, given how often they report them going off.

A few weeks ago I came upon a bow hunter, a retired Scottsdale police officer on this same stretch of road. He had been hunting in this area for years. He told us the Border Patrol had told him after tracking him one day that he had set off a sensor. Two weeks earlier while walking north on a trail for about half an hour off this same road, my two companions and I headed back south to our truck and came around a bend. There stood six Border Patrol agents lined up on the trail. They all looked quite disappointed to see three gringos. One in our group was wearing tennis shoes, and the lead tracker asked to see the bottom of her shoes. "Yeah, that's them," he said.

This same bow hunter said the area was dangerous, drug runners and such coming through. He was wearing a .45 at his side. He told us about a bloody mattress at the bottom of a ravine, about a fifty-pound pack of marijuana that he discovered over a year ago only two miles from there. He had reported its precise location with GPS technology to the Border Patrol and sheriff's department, and yet the pot was still sitting there to this day.

We head north on the trail to where the trees have been pruned nicely to provide a nice opening to pass. We look for antennas poking out of the trees. We go back to the truck and begin to drive back to the pavement. About a quarter mile down, a Border Patrol unit is parked on the shoulder of the road with no agent on board. Did we set off a sensor? How the hell are we supposed to know? But that's right—we're not supposed to know.

Back on the highway we head south, and the radio crackles again. Seems something is up near milepost 13, but the message is garbled and we do not hear clearly. We see a red compact car that had run off the road and tried to do a little four-wheeling. It looked like a shark out of water, sitting fifty yards off the two-lane highway in the middle of the desert. We come around a curve, where four Border Patrol units have an older model Chevy pickup penned in. As we slowly cruise by, the false bottom is being lifted up, the dark-haired occupants begin to rise. We stop and inquire if we may offer food and water, and the agent in charge says, "No, we're fine. You move on."

We arrive in Arivaca. Three Border Patrol units are parked at the mercantile. We cruise slowly out to the highway, and three miles outside of town I spot Fabian on a hill, working his way toward the road. He's about two hundred yards from the highway in low scrub with no cover. He watches me approach and walks toward me. "Hello friend, I have food and water," I say. "Would you like some?"

"Yes, I am thirsty." He looks at me like I am a human being.

"How long have you been out here walking?"

"Four days."

"What happened?"

"They left me while I was sleeping."

"Do you want to go back to the border, to Nogales?"

"Yes, I do."

"Where are you from?"

"Veracruz."

He takes a long, slow pull of the water I have given him. "We will call the Border Patrol and they will take you back," I say.

"Which way is Mexico?" he asks.

I show him. He is completely turned around. He thought it was to the east. He looks relieved to know where he has come from. To know where you are in the world in relation to the people you love is comforting. Not to know can be torture.

We give him a flyer that shows where there is shelter for migrants in Nogales, Sonora, which is where he will most likely be deported. Before our call to Border Patrol goes through, a little Border Patrol jeep happens by and stops. The agent gets out.

"He wants to go home," I tell him.

The agent motions for Fabian to come with him. I don't think he will go home. I think he will rest up and try again, as most of them do. They will continue to try and get across until they make it, are jailed as repeat offenders, go back home, or die trying.

My young friend asks me if Fabian knows Alfonso, since they were both from Veracruz. That makes me laugh. He also wants to know why people are left behind when they go to sleep. I don't know.

Story Ten

~ TED

Today is a day for our cause to marshal the forces of the media. I don't realize it at first, but it is soon to be in the forefront of my consciousness. I receive a message from the person who schedules trips advising me that a young woman in our group will be leading an ABC weekend news team on our outing into the desert. They're doing a story on migrants and the support Christian groups are giving them.

I meet a familiar face at the shed. He has already loaded the truck. The young woman shows at 7:00 a.m., apologizing for being an hour late. The ABC crew calls her cell phone and lets us know they are running late as well. Something about breakfast not being served quickly enough.

The sun is now climbing higher into the sky, and I begin to get antsy. We are usually on the highway by now between the ranges that ring our patrol route, and to be sitting at the shed is disquieting. The ABC crew arrives, driving a big black SUV that looks as if the Secret Service uses it for a presidential detail. It is packed with all types of equipment for making the news.

They most certainly want to make it, as does a second crew, which mysteriously appears on the scene. The second group is from the Discovery Channel, and the producer is letting the young woman know in no uncertain terms that her news team has permission and was told it was "cool" to follow us.

Already I can feel the animosity between the two news groups. The ABC group feels like the Discovery Channel is poaching their story, and they are the heavy hitters. No? The woman who is producing for the Discovery Channel will not back down and begins to plead. It is quickly turning into a scene, and so I broach a compromise: we will meet the Discovery Channel people at high noon at the mercantile in Arivaca, and they can follow along at that point. By then the ABC crew will have all they need to make their story, or so I hope.

We leave the shed finally about two hours later than what we should have and head out Route 86. We are to meet the ABC crew in Three Points. They have already told us they want to set up a camera inside the Samaritan truck to get shots of the young woman driving. The producer will be interviewing her during this segment. We get to Three Points, the crew sets up a camera inside our truck, and we head south. They ask me to ride in the big black SUV, which has enough air-conditioning for three cars. The sound person in the rear puts on her jacket to stay warm. We pull in at a ranch road, drive down a few miles, and find fresh tracks of footprints crossing the road. We pull down a side road and move back into the bush, where the camera crew, along with the Samaritans, walk south on a trail. They film her calling out into the desert. We see no one and go back to the trucks.

We load up and head farther south and go onto another ranch road. We see some tracks. We briefly consider going down a very narrow single-lane road, but the camera guy doesn't want to. He's worried about brush scratching his big black SUV.

We see a Border Patrol truck parked on the side of the road with not a soul in it. Someone has put a note on the windshield wipers. I ask them to stop, and I check it out. The note is from the National Refuge ranger. It says that migrants were spotted crossing the road down by the windmill at 9:00 a.m. It's now 10:15. I don't tell the news crew what the note says. I don't want to find any migrants on this road with a full news crew and the Border Patrol nearby.

Continuing on to a lake, the crew sets up to do an interview with the young Samaritan. I remind her that we need to meet the other crew in town soon, and she lets me know that she is not interested in helping them out. I remind her what is at stake here. Whether she wants to or not, we need to meet them, since we have the opportunity to make two stories in one day.

She needs to realize what the big picture is; it is important for our story to reach as many people as possible, and we have an opportunity here. We will make the news with the other crew, period. She seems to understand.

The ABC people finish the interview, and the camera guy wants to do some trick movie shots using a side-mount camera. Then we head into town.

We find the Discovery Channel crew at the mercantile. We're an hour late, but they're not upset, since while they waited two migrants walked up and used the phone, purchased some sodas, and then walked away. They got them on tape. I tell them we will take them to a spot where migrants often pass through and rest. It is only a couple of miles away, and they can get some footage of us calling out to the empty desert. I invite the ABC news crew along, but they're not interested.

We go to a place near the road and give the Discovery Channel crew ground rules. If we run into anyone, we must get permission first to photograph and interview him or her. The camera guy follows us around, the lens pointing in my face and the faces of my fellow Samaritans as we tromp through the brush and call out. We come across a number of camps. We have been calling out for half an hour when I hear someone return my call. Six men from Veracruz appear, haggard. I can tell they don't really know what to make of me when the reporter for Discovery walks up and in rapid-fire Spanish tells them who she is and what they are doing and if it would be all right to photograph and interview them. I did not know that she's bilingual, and I find out later that the cameraman, her husband, is fluent as well. The six from Veracruz shake their heads in unison, yes it would be okay, and then I ask each one individually if they are sure and each says yes again.

The six have been separated from their guide, or so they say. One in the group speaks English pretty well and appears to be the leader. He has a very modern haircut. All six are going to North Carolina. One is fifteen years old and is going to be reunited with his mother and father, whom he has not seen in five years. The leader, named Lorenzo, has a wife and child there. He says he has worked as a painter in and around Raleigh. We offer them food and water and they take it. I ask if they would like to use a phone, and they call family in North Carolina to let them know they are safe at the moment.

The camera operator and sound guy start shooting us and the migrants, and the producer begins to interview Lorenzo, and when they are done with him they interview others in the party.

A Black Hawk helicopter we have been hearing now comes into view. It has been circling the general area but is too far away, I think, to spot us. Still, it's time to go. The producer gives the six some money, and then they turn and move away, heading up the hill toward the road and what they are hoping is their ride.

Out on the highway we come to a roadblock. The Border Patrol asks if we are citizens, the only thing they can ask unless they have probable cause. We answer yes.

A few weeks later I'm sitting in a local restaurant, and a couple of the boys in the kitchen tell me they saw me on television in a show about migrants. They are undocumented Mexicans, and they were watching the Spanish-language version of the Discovery Channel. I ask them if they enjoyed the show, and they say yes. Some Samaritans making the news.

Norma

Photograph by Kathryn Ferguson

Previous page: Crosses on border wall represent migrant deaths in Tucson Sector.

Story Eleven

I never met Lucresia, but her father, a kind and grateful man, occupies a unique niche in our community and a special place in our hearts. We became friends with Cesario during the several weeks he spent in Tucson while he made daily treks into the desert to search for Lucresia's body. It was early July, before the rains arrived, and the daytime temperatures were sweltering. I received a call from a person at Derechos Humanos, the human rights organization here in Tucson, who said a Mexican man had arrived in Tucson to search for his daughter. He asked if we, the Samaritans, could help. I recommended that they also contact one of the other volunteer organizations, No More Deaths (NMD), whose volunteers were camped in the desert near the border. Twice daily they made trips into the washes, into the cactus and creosote thickets, looking for migrants in need or in distress. Samaritans made daily trips from Tucson into the desert, driving along the highways and rutted four-wheel-drive roads and hiking the migrant trails. We would search those routes.

Thus Cesario was introduced to the Tucson volunteer community, and the community came to embrace him and became endeared to him.

Cesario's daughter Lucresia had left her home, a small town in northern Zacatecas, Mexico, to come north with her children so they could reunite with husband and father to make a better life. Her fifteen-year-old son and seven-year-old daughter made the trip with her. They were able to tolerate the harsh conditions of the Sonoran Desert much better than their mother. Lucresia found it very difficult at first and then impossible to keep up with her group. As they pushed on, she became more dehydrated. Finally, unable to continue, she sent her daughter on with the rest of the group. Her son, Jesús, stayed with her. He built a fire to signal for help, but none came.

Jesús did all he could for Lucresia, and as she drank the last drop from their water jugs he went in search of water and help. Two days later the Border Patrol found him, lost and wandering in the dry desert scrub. He told them he left his mother behind and begged them to go in search of her. They were unable to locate the spot where the son had left his mother. Jesús was then deported back to Mexico, or "voluntarily returned," as it is recorded when the border crosser voluntarily agrees to return to Mexico. However, the Border Patrol had no legal authority to voluntarily return Jesús, since he was a minor. He was flown to Mexico City, then sent by bus to Zacatecas, his home state.

Cesario had heard from a person connected to the migrant smuggling ring that his daughter had become ill on the journey. An unknown person, possibly the coyote, called Lucresia's husband in Texas and told him about the mother and son left in the desert. The husband called his family in Zacatecas, and they told Lucresia's family. Cesario got on a bus and headed for the border. The father was determined to find the remains of his daughter. He knew that in the desert heat the body would not remain intact for very long, but he was determined to find her. Two friends joined to help; one had lived in the states for many years and spoke English. These two men would accompany him on his search.

Cesario made contact with volunteers at the NMD camp, and they in turn contacted a pilot who had worked with Samaritans in the past. She volunteered the use of her plane and spent a day flying Cesario and one of his friends over the Altar Valley to get an overview of the terrain and perhaps see something that would provide a clue. By the end of that day, the two men grasped the vastness of the Arizona desert and the monotony of vegetation. They realized the futility of trying to find a body or a pile of bones by searching from the air. Now Cesario knew that he had to search the desert on foot.

After he had been returned home, Jesús made contact with his grandfather. Now he wanted to come to Arizona to join Cesario's search for his mother's body and to help locate the spot where he left his mother's side. Cesario sent for his grandson, hoping the teenager would be able to find the place he had last seen his mother. Once at the border, Cesario requested a special permit to allow the boy to stay in the United States long enough to aid with the search. An attorney made petition to have the young boy paroled to stay in the United States in custody, just long enough to help with the search, but this was denied. Attempts to have bond granted so he could aid in the search were also futile. Border Patrol met Jesús at the border, and with five agents Jesús was driven around to several possible sites. He did not recognize any of the surroundings. The day's search unsuccessful, the boy was returned to the Mexican side of the border and was refused permission to return to the United States.

Cesario and his two friends would have to search blindly, armed only with the information Jesús could give about landmarks in the vicinity of where he had left his mother. So the grandson stayed in Nogales, Mexico, and all day his grandfather Cesario and two companions searched and took photos of the locations where they traveled. Late each day he would have the photos developed at a one-hour developer and take the pictures to show Jesús, hoping that the boy would see a familiar landmark that would help them in their search. So the nightly ritual repeated itself: grandfather and grandson would meet across the border looking at the photos, discarding some and saving those that showed familiar landmarks.

In Nogales, Sonora, the owners of a hotel learned about the search for Lucresia's body. They took Jesús under their wing, providing free lodging and food for the teenager and teaching him English and the business of hotel administration. Cesario's two sons and friends of his sons sent cell phones, a van to drive, and money for gas. In California the sons contacted a Spanish-language radio station and related the story. That radio station passed the information along to a Spanish-language station in Tucson, and both stations raised money to help in the effort.

The search continued for three weeks. During that time Cesario and his companions three times found remains of other bodies. Each one found raised hope that this would be Lucresia, but he never saw anything that he identified as belonging to his daughter. The clothes were in rags and the bodies had deteriorated beyond recognition; so he looked around the remains for any of the jewelry that she wore. He remembered how she never took off her Virgin of Guadalupe ring; for her it was an amulet to keep her safe. The three men also assisted many other border crossers. When they encountered migrants, they would help them with directions, food, or water, and if the migrants wanted to turn back they would call the Border Patrol to pick them up. If they needed attention to blisters or other minor first-aid needs, the men would call one of the volunteer groups.

Cesario did not at first think that the last body they found was his daughter's. He wasn't sure about the surrounding landmarks that Jesús had mentioned, and he did not recognize any clothing. They called the sheriff, as they had done when finding the previous three bodies. The sheriff's team saw an American flag tied to a tree branch close by.

A person who had been in the group traveling with Lucresia had sent word to Cesario that an American flag had been seen near her body. They found a hand near the skull. On the left hand were three rings, including a pinkie ring with an image of the Virgin of Guadalupe. His search was over.

During his month in Tucson, Cesario made many friends. The motel where he stayed accommodated him without charge, a nearby Mexican restaurant fed him gratis, and members of No More Deaths, Derechos Humanos, and Samaritans helped Cesario in his search.

The day after the search ended, several volunteers along with Father Ricardo, a priest in Tucson active in social justice causes, held a service at the site where the body was found and planted a cross there as a shrine to Lucresia. A memorial service was held at St. Mark's Presbyterian Church before her remains were shipped back to Mexico.

Lucresia's daughter, Nora, arrived safely and reunited with her father in Texas. Before Cesario left, there was a potluck dinner at Southside church for him and his friend. It was a sad occasion, but there was a spirit of triumph among the assembled group of humanitarian volunteers and social activists. This quiet, humble man had told his friend, "If I find her I know it will be just a pile of bones, but I want to find her. I want to bury my daughter in her country."

Lucresia returned home to Zacatecas. She left those of us in Tucson a legacy of renewal in our determination to do everything we can to prevent the deaths in the desert, to aid desert crossers in distress. Lucresia symbolizes what is bequeathed to families by this diaspora: separation and destruction of the family unit, pain and death—all in search of a better job and better way of life.

Story Twelve

Isabel hobbled toward me as she made her way on crutches down the hospital corridor. She wore an inexplicable large grin for someone with one broken ankle and the other ankle severely sprained. She was very overweight, but this did not slow her down as she moved rapidly on her *muletas*. It had taken me all afternoon to locate her. Bethia had called me from the Green Valley Samaritan patrol. They had found eighteen-year-old Isabel in an isolated area where the *pollero* and rest of the group had deserted her. Bethia called the Border Patrol, who told her to call 911. She told me that Isabel was en route to a Tucson hospital and asked me to follow up and find out where and what treatment the young woman had received.

The severity of bruising on both of her legs was extreme. Her right thigh was a blotched purple and blue. Her left leg reminded me of a Monet painting, nothing but blues, mauves, and purples in a myopic blur. She had one sprained and one fractured ankle, but the sprained one was more swollen and painful than the broken one. I am sure that her obesity and lack of physical fitness contributed to her repeatedly falling. She had tried to keep up with her group but stumbled again and again as they went uphill, downhill, and up again. She said she felt like one of those giant boulders rolling down the hill as she slipped and slid, trying to keep up with the group. Then she fell with one leg doubled behind the other, like a pretzel.

When she arrived at the hospital, the medical attendant had cut the legs of her jeans up above her knees in order to apply splints. I went to the thrift store to get something for her to wear and got a couple of size 18 dresses, but one was too small. Isabel told her story of coming to the United States. She was traveling with a group of twenty. Just before they crossed the border the coyote made a call on his cell phone. He then told them to cross and continue without him, he would meet up with them later at an appointed location. He pointed out the trail, well worn and easy to follow. Many feet had traveled that path headed toward bright dreams, hopes, and promises of reuniting with loved ones. After the group reached the American side, it came to an open area like a gravel pit. The group was to sleep there and meet up with the coyote the following day.

The crossers had not been at that location long when a gang of banditos arrived. At gunpoint the thieves took everyone's money and forced the women to line up and strip off all clothing. As the queue of women stood there naked, a bandit walked up to one, leaned into her face with a sneer, and began first stroking, then squeezing her breasts. As if on cue, his comrade came up behind a teenage girl and began rubbing up against her buttocks and running his hand up the inside of her thighs. The women dropped their heads. They stared at the ground, refusing to look at the *ladrones*. Some of the women began to sob, tears falling on the dusty ground. The aura of shame and degradation crowded out their fear. But not Isabel. When the other women started to disrobe, the intruders said to her, "Never mind." She must have wondered if she had been spared the terrible humiliation because of her obesity.

The next morning their pollero rejoined the group to guide them north to meet their pickup vehicle. Isabel stumbled and fell more than the previous days. When the pollero realized that she couldn't keep up, he pointed toward a road. He told her to wait there, and probably someone would come by and help. The rest of the group continued its journey. She had not known any of her fellow travelers, but they were sympathetic, and one woman offered to contact her family in Mexico.

She had waited beside the road, and that was where the Green Valley Samaritans found her.

I returned to the hospital with a cardigan sweater, underwear, and toiletries. There was no shampoo in the hospital bathroom, so I brought a small bottle, a comb and brush, and clips for her hair. She thanked me, then her round face again lit up with a smile as she told us about contacting her mother back home in Mexico. None of the family had known what had happened to Isabel, and although her mother was upset about the injuries, she was thankful her daughter was alive. The mother had not wanted Isabel to go *al otro lado*, to the other side, but there was no work available in their hometown, and a cousin in Georgia had promised to help find a job for her. Isabel now works in Atlanta. She is healthy but needs more surgery on her ankle. She is afraid that if she takes medical time off she will lose her job. "Más tarde," she said. "Later I will have the operation."

Story Thirteen

It was mid-January when we arrived very early at the Mariposa port of entry on the border. We zipped our jackets snug for warmth, and I wrapped my wool scarf tightly, hoping to stop my teeth from chattering. Two other Samaritans and I had driven the sixty-five miles from Tucson to bring supplies and to assist the local volunteer workers there. The men were preparing hot soup, and a large urn of hot coffee sat on the table in front of the tent. Migrants who have been expelled from the U.S. side of the border by Border Patrol trek down the path alongside the cyclone fence. When they reach the end of the walkway they are in Mexico. Home? Not really. Most are from farther south and have to decide whether to try again to cross or give up and return to their local communities. No More Deaths has established and runs an aid station right at the border, on the Mexican side. The Commission for Protection of Migrants, established by the Mexican state of Sonora, helps in overseeing the daily function of the aid station, and volunteers from Green Valley Samaritans and Tucson Samaritans come down to volunteer as well.

That morning the three of us joined the three young Mexican men who staffed the tent to attend to the needs of the ejected border crossers. That is, as best they could with the limited supplies they have. We were bringing food and cups for drinks and soup. I had brought medical supplies and planned to use my own rather than deplete the bandage materials that are kept there for use. Already a busload of fifty migrants had passed through. Some did not stop at the tent, but most wanted the hot liquids to warm their cold bodies and souls.

Most of the busloads of people were "voluntary returnees," migrants who signed papers that they were voluntarily going back, and thus avoiding incarceration, court, and formal deportation. This option is only available to Mexican migrants—those from other countries do not have this choice. Many of the Central and South American migrants carry false Mexican identification papers. They hope that if they are apprehended here in the Arizona desert, they will not be sent back to their home country, but will be taken to the Mexican border, released, and they can then turn around and try again to cross.

After being apprehended by the Border Patrol, migrants are held in custody twelve to eighteen hours, often without food or water during this time. It is not unusual for them to be detained much longer, even up to four days. Unless a serious medical condition is apparent, no medical attention is administered, and frequently they tell us that their medications have been taken away and not returned.

Occasionally at the aid station a serious medical situation necessitates sending a returnee to the hospital; but the most frequent ailment, in addition to dehydration, is blisters. Sometimes people deny any problem even though removal of shoes and socks reveals blisters on the balls of the foot and between toes, and other times we can see them limping as they walk toward us. It is not unusual to see one or two fellow travelers holding a person's arm, assisting him or her, because blisters on the bottom of the foot can be like a severe burn.

One of the top requests at the tent was for shoelaces. We'd see groups of people approaching our station with tennis shoes open, walking in a sort of shuffling gate to keep their shoes from falling off. The Border Patrol always confiscated the shoelaces and belts, and most of the time they were not returned.

Lorenzo's feet were in that middle range, blistered but not enough to cause him to limp. The day had warmed up as the clouds disappeared, and flies swarmed around the piled-up garbage twenty feet away across the street. Lorenzo sat in front of the tent in the sun soaking one foot, while I cleaned and bandaged the other. We talked about his family. It was good practice for my Spanish comprehension. Because he had worked in the United States for the past three years, we were able to communicate, even though he spoke only a few words of English. He had been working in the lumber industry in California, but had gone home to his pueblo in Campeche for Christmas. His return was typical of the trip of many workers who do not return until after January 6, Día de los Reyes, remaining with their families for all the seasonal celebrations. Campeche is one of the states on the Yucatán Peninsula of Mexico. Tourists are familiar with the state of Quintana Roo, on the eastern side of the peninsula, where the vacation town of Cancún is located. The state of Campeche is on the western side.

Migrants return to Mexico via Mariposa port of entry after release from Border Patrol custody.

I asked what kind of work he had done in his hometown. "Mecánico," he said. I expressed surprise that having skill in a trade, he would leave family and come so far to work. He told me that he made ten dollars a day. This was not sufficient to support his family, and to complicate matters his five-year-old son had a serious medical condition. The son was born with congenital ptosis of the eyelids, the inability to raise his eyelids. Lorenzo demonstrated the way his son had to tilt his head back in order to see. He said that the child had been to Mexico City for corrective surgery. The surgeons had taken a nerve from the side of the leg of the boy's mother and had transplanted it to the boy's eyelids. This was to give him the ability to raise and lower his eyelids. Although the condition was improved, the child could only partially open his eyes. Lorenzo said they did not have enough money to take him back to Mexico City for a follow-up visit after surgery. He attributed the lack of complete success to the incomplete follow-up care.

I wanted to do something, anything, to help. I felt a tightness in my chest and throat and the backs of my jaws were burning, right behind my teeth. I felt so powerless. As a mother and grandmother, I could feel the tug between leaving home to better provide for your family and the longing to stay and provide comfort, love, and support.

The description of the nerve transplant puzzled me. I was not familiar with the diagnosis, and I did not realize that nerves could be transplanted. This was far from my field of medical training and also not a
subject that was covered in the medical literature that I regularly review.
I knew that there had been a great deal of research in the field of nerve
regeneration, which had been greatly supported by the late actor Chris-
topher Reeve after the injury that resulted in his quadriplegia.

Later that week I met a new Samaritan volunteer who told me he
was a retired plastic surgeon and answered my question, saying the surgery that had been performed was a fascial transplant. Fascia is the
connective tissue found throughout the body, especially around muscles. Lorenzo had mistakenly thought that tissue taken from his wife's
leg was nerve tissue, a reasonable assumption since the surgery was
intended to improve movement of the eyelids.

It was difficult to get Lorenzo and his son out of my mind. I called
a friend in another state, also a plastic surgeon, whom I had not seen or
talked to in ten years. Harvey and I had worked together on many cases
when I was practicing oncology. We frequently consulted each other
about patients with breast cancer. He performed breast reconstruction
after mastectomy, and I treated the patient with chemotherapy or other
medical management of the cancer.

Right away he knew and explained to me the nuances of the eye
condition. He said that even though the eyelids could not be raised due
to a congenital absence of the levator muscles of the eyelids, there was
a two- or three-millimeter opening between the upper and lower lids so
that a patient could tilt the head backward to see. The fascia that would
be transplanted would attach the eyelids to the muscles of the forehead.
The patient could then wrinkle up the brow as if to raise the eyebrows,
and this would raise the upper lids. This was far from giving a patient
normal functioning eyelid muscles, but it would allow for better vision
without always tilting back his head.

Then Harvey said, "I've heard about all the humanitarian work on
the border. It is wonderful that people there in Arizona are so compassionate toward migrants." He added, "I never call them aliens. My father
was an illegal immigrant for twenty-five years." I had never known this.
He had often laughed about wanting to learn Yiddish from his parents,
but his father would say, "We're American, we speak English!"—except
when the parents didn't want the children to know what they were
saying.

"My grandfather was imprisoned in Poland because he wouldn't
fight for the tsar," Harvey said. "What Jew would want to fight for the

tsar? But my grandfather was a tough old guy, and after he escaped from prison, he was smuggled across eastern Europe, then to Canada. From there he crossed into Detroit. He worked for five years, saving money to bring his wife and children from Europe. As a youth, my father hated Poland and Europe. He was a blond, blue-eyed kid, and the other school kids used to tease him and say his mother had been raped by a Cossack. My grandfather finally got enough money, but the week before the family was to come, the United States changed the legal quotas and they were denied admission. My grandfather paid for them to come to Canada, and then my grandmother with my father and his two siblings were smuggled across the Ambassador Bridge over the Detroit River into the United States. He grew up and married my mother, a U.S.-born citizen.

"My uncle, my father's younger brother, grew up to become a paratrooper and was in the 101st Airborne. He died at Normandy. My father was too old to be drafted in World War II, so he worked in a munitions factory. Because of my mother's American-born status, he could have applied for citizenship, but he was afraid it might not be granted. After the war, all the noncitizen soldiers who had fought and all those who had worked in the defense industry were granted amnesty. I remember in 1948 going to the federal building when he was sworn in as a U.S. citizen.

"But back to the young boy with the eye problem," Harvey said. "There is a lot of research and new corrective procedures are on the horizon." He told me that there is stem cell research on regenerating nerve tissue and muscle tissue.

I didn't really feel any better after talking with him. I doubted that the new procedures would be available to Lorenzo's son.

After I bandaged his feet, I gave Lorenzo a plastic bag with extra bandage material and instructed him how to use it. I told him to keep his feet dry and change his socks if they got wet. We handed him two pairs of new, thick socks to take with him. He turned and handed one pair to one of the buddies waiting on him. The three fellow travelers had been drinking hot soup in the tent and now were laughing in the warm sun, telling jokes as they waited on Lorenzo to leave.

I asked Lorenzo what he would do now. "Voy a volver a Altar," he said matter-of-factly. "I'm going back to Altar," the jumping-off place for crossing the Mexico-Arizona border. The place to connect again with a coyote. He would continue to cross until he made it to California.

Story Fourteen

The tan Jeep Cherokee drove at patrol speed heading south on Route 286, the north–south secondary road that parallels the border of the Tohono O'odham Nation land for forty-seven miles leading to the U.S.–Mexican border town of Sasabe. Looking east from here you can see the jagged horizon of the Cerro Colorado, an imposing mountain range, in the distance. But that day in July, the landscape linking those mountains with this highway was scorched and dry. Our Samaritan vehicle tried to maintain a speed between 40 and 45 mph. We did not want to miss seeing any migrant who needed help.

Migrants are difficult to spot, with their brown skin, dark clothes, dark backpacks, and baseball caps. They move quietly through the scrub. Along most of this road the mesquite trees are not dense, and there are not many of the tall saguaro cacti in this valley, but the unvarying nature of the landscape here helps to camouflage traveling migrants. No one—not the Border Patrol, the Samaritans, or the Minutemen— can spot them easily. The Border Patrol utilizes movement sensors, heat sensors, helicopters, horse patrols, agents on ATVs and dirt bikes. Still, between 1,000 and 1,500 people a day in the Tucson Sector alone make it through the gauntlet, according to most estimates.

At first glance the terrain here is monotonous, almost monochromatic. You have to observe this land quietly without regard to time. Just sit still and watch lizards, packrats, birds, and rabbits. See the huge red-tailed hawks sitting on pole after pole along Route 286. Gaze at the western mountains at sunrise when the eastern sky is crimson and Baboquivari Peak is bathed in a pinkish glow. Then look east at sunset toward those lavender mountains etched with maroon shadows. Watch in the evening as the sun smears the western sky with strokes of pink, turquoise, gold, and mauve. Listen to the hoarse wind as it blows across fields dotted by cacti and squatty trees. Then you will fall in love with this place. The mesquite trees, most of which do not stand over ten feet high, and scrubby bushes are punctuated by prickly pear cacti and barbed spines of the cholla cactus. This landscape holds many deceptions. At any time of day a prickly pear can catch the angle of the sun and reflect it in such a way that a person surveying the horizon would not recognize it as vegetation, instead thinking it a signal, a discarded item, or even a person. The cholla cacti, when spotted at a distance, especially on a ridge, give the illusion of someone on the move. It takes binoculars, or a few moments of study to be able to discern that it is not human.

Of the four occupants in the vehicle, three of us were medical and one a Salvadorean teacher studying at the University of Arizona. One of the nurses and the teacher had never been on patrol before. We were glad to have him along to contribute his translating skills. Two of us spoke halting Spanish, and his company was especially welcomed.

The jeep pulled off onto the shoulder of the road to allow others to pass. There was only an occasional passing vehicle, usually a truck. At times when traffic was heavier along this stretch of highway you could see as many Mexican as Arizona license plates going in both directions. As we pulled back onto the pavement, we saw in the distance, on the opposite side of the road coming toward us, a lone figure pushing a bicycle. As we got closer, we could tell that the young man in jeans and dark sweatshirt was moving very slowly. Both bicycle tires were flat, and his backpack was slung over the handlebars. Occasionally we had seen discarded bicycles in the brush on the roadside. I had wondered then if a migrant had cycled up from the border until he got a ride. Had the Border Patrol apprehended him, forcing him to abandon the bicycle?

Once two Samaritans returned from patrol with a dented bicycle in the back of the SUV. They said they had not seen any migrants who needed help but had medically evacuated a bicycle from the desert. Several years ago in Alamos, Sonora, I had talked with a young man who was working in a restaurant there. When he heard of our volunteer work with the migrants in the desert, he told his story. He had come up the same route that we were driving on that day. His cousin had obtained two bicycles, and the young men would ride at night and hide during the daytime. If headlights were seen approaching, they would drag the bikes over into some brush or a ditch to hide. They made it all the way to Phoenix and then took a bus to Colorado. After saving some money, he returned home.

Now, reflecting on his story, and having seen all those rejected bicycles along this route in the past, I wondered if someone in Sasabe was making a fortune in bicycle sales. Or did the young man in front of us take advantage of someone's carelessness at leaving a bicycle unsecured? We did not ask where he got the bicycle. Our purpose was to provide food, water, and medical care.

We rolled down the car window and called out, "¿Hola, necesita ayuda? ¿Necesita agua o comida?" Our familiar refrain.

We pulled off the pavement, and the teacher and a nurse got out and crossed the road to the young man. He nodded in response to their questions and began gesturing with his hands, pointing to his feet and his mouth. The two instructed him to move off the road and lean the bicycle against a small mesquite tree. The wind was blowing dust and dried brush, and across the desert scrub you could see dust devils, like small tan tornadoes moving along the horizon. The threesome huddled in shrubbery, protected from the wind. He nodded his head in response to other questions, using hand motions and gestures. He did not respond verbally to any of their questions, and then they realized he was unable to talk. He made motions as if writing on a pad of paper, and the teacher pulled out paper and a pen from his backpack. He nodded and wrote, "Comida, por favor."

The nurse inquired about his feet "¿Tiene ampollas? ¿Le duelen los pies? ¿Tiene agua?"

He made hand gestures and nodded in response to each question, and then he held up a gallon jug half full of cloudy water with brownish sediment in the bottom. The teacher told the young man to discard the water, explaining that the dirty water would cause sickness and that we had plenty of water for him. Many migrants become sick from drinking cattle-tank water. Then the vomiting and diarrhea begin, which intensifies their dehydration and can lead to kidney failure.

The teacher repeated the inquiry about his feet and asked if there were other medical problems.

As they sat in grass and rocks there on the roadside, the nurse helped him remove his badly worn shoes. We saw that the sole of the left shoe had come unsewn and the heel had come off. His feet had large, fluid-filled blisters covering the pads of the soles of both feet. The puffy, white skin that looked like fluid-filled pouches extended between his toes. As the nurse cleaned and bandaged his feet, he watched her movements intently as she reached into the medical bag time and again for antiseptic, antibiotic ointment, gauze, and tape. As the teacher continued talking to him in fluent Spanish, the traveling patient was observing every movement of his Florence Nightingale. He looked inside the medical bag, pulled out the stethoscope, and held it to her back. He pretended to be listening to the nurse's breathing, as she tended to his wounded feet. Then with a mischievous grin, he spoke to the humanitarians.

They looked up in surprise. He was not really mute. Now he abandoned his charade. Speaking to the teacher in Spanish, he told how terrified he had been the previous night. Just after dark he had heard a pack of coyotes howl. Fearful, he climbed up a scrawny mesquite tree and perched in the fork of two branches where he spent the night. He said all night he could hear the coyotes. Though they do not usually pose a danger to people, he was convinced that the coyotes had circled the tree all night, howling until daybreak. Now, in the daylight of mid-morning, his grin and twinkling dark eyes contradicted fear. His smile was more than just warm and appealing. Charisma beamed out of the creases around his mouth and eyes, and we were all ensnared.

He told us he had crossed the border alone two days earlier, trying to make his way on his own. No group, no *pollero*. He had come all the way from Nicaragua, his home, where he had grown up an orphan on the streets. Both parents had been killed in the wars while fighting for the Sandinistas, the leftist army that overthrew the dictatorship in Nicaragua and was opposed by the U.S.-backed Contras. His middle name was Mao. As a teenager on the streets, he had run with gangs that took drugs and used alcohol. Now in his twenties, he wanted to come to the United States to get a decent job and earn an honest wage. He had a brother in California and wanted to join him and try work there in construction, or landscaping, or maybe in a restaurant.

His first name, he said, was Angel. I said "Oh, AHN-hel," the Spanish pronunciation. He shook his head, "No, Angel," he replied. Maybe he was absorbing a new sense of self, of being, of place. The concept of where he was and where he belonged was changing. Perhaps that is why he dropped the pretense of being mute. He began to trust us.

Ted

Photograph by Kathryn Ferguson

Previous page: In Sasabe, Mexico, a crucifix looks into the United States with distant Baboquivari Peak guiding the way north.

Story Fifteen

It is early June, and we have been blessed by rain in the desert. We had received only half an inch until yesterday, when the clouds marched strong and fast into the Tucson basin and left one third of an inch of rain, almost equaling the total for the year so far. Of course, it was only recorded out at the airport, this third of an inch of rain. Downtown received a smattering, just enough to dirty up a freshly washed car. But such is the way of summer rain in this part of the world. You get what you get and you don't complain, since water from the clouds is manna from heaven.

We are leaving this afternoon for Mexico, and the big white puffy clouds with blue-black bottoms are gathering. Our destination is a border town of fewer than a thousand people, not counting the migrants.

There we will go to a brickyard called Ladrillal, the final staging area for migrants and *narcotraficantes*. Here the migrants will wait for their guides or runners to lead them over the border. The brickyard is five miles south of the border and is so far removed from the central governments of Washington and Mexico City that it might as well be on Mars. Burnt adobe bricks were made here from the red loamy clay and fired in big ovens. This is one of the reasons the town of Sasabe exists and the port of entry maintained, so these bricks could be transported easily north in great quantities to build homes. The brickyard is no longer in operation, or so I've been told, but many homes in Tucson and Phoenix were built with the bricks that came from this place, each one stamped with "Mexico" on the wide side.

This port of entry in reality encompasses a fifty-mile east-to-west border of desert between the two countries, with Sasabe at its center. Goods flow north mostly in the form of humans and illegal drugs, and in return stolen cars, guns, and U.S. dollars head south. Although the port is officially open only between the hours of 8:00 a.m. and 8:00 p.m., most of the goods are moved during the hours it is closed, along the myriad trails and nameless jeep tracks that cross the line between the two countries.

The town itself is isolated from the interior of Mexico by the fact that there are only two roads leading to it. One is a very poorly maintained dirt road called "la brecha" that meanders ninety-one kilometers south to the town of Altar. On the other side of the border a two-lane highway heads north, and in an hour you can be in Tucson. It has been reported that more than 1,500 migrants a day arrive at the brickyard awaiting the cover of darkness to move north.

Our mission today is to provide these migrants with food, water, hats, socks, and shoes. As we approach the border the U.S. customs facility has the appearance of a Swiss chalet. As you get closer, it retains this profile, but you can see the structure is just a series of blue peaked roofs used to create shade for the inspection bays, a booth, and a brick building that houses what I'm not sure. The gate that separates the two countries is just a cattle guard wide enough for two small cars and a simple swinging gate. A four-strand barbed-wire fence heads off to the east and west. This is the legal port of entry.

We cross over and stop at Mexican customs, and a man comes out and checks our truck. He wants to know where we are going with all the supplies. My partner says we are taking all the water to Grupo Beta. He asks about the shoes and socks and my partner says they will be given to them as well. He waves us through, and we head down the dirt road into town.

We pass the building where Grupo Beta has its offices and continue on. We are not on an official visit and do not want the protection of this Mexican government agency, set up ostensibly to help the migrants. Its mission is murky, and its trucks are all brand new and have colorful yellow paint jobs. We see some *federales* in camouflage walking into a store. We cross a wash and go through the only stretch of paved road in Sasabe. The town is deserted. There's not a soul on the street during the hottest part of the day.

We continue through town and head south past a graveyard and then a baseball field and out into the Sonoran Desert toward the brickyard. The road is as washboard as can be, and my truck rattles so loudly that my partner and I have to yell to speak with each other.

After fifteen minutes we come to a crossroads with a small house on the corner made of red burnt adobe bricks and turn right. We drive down the road and scattered here and there are small houses, all made of this red brick and surrounded by what appears to be a junkyard. This junkyard stretches from home to home for more than half a mile. Most of the parts and pieces are of one or two models only, vans and pickup trucks, mainly Fords in various states of repair and disrepair. These are the vehicles that will bring the migrant the final few miles to the jumping-off trailheads that head north.

We stop at a small store, a *tienda*. It is basically a shack with an open window looking into a few shelves filled with last-minute items the migrant might need. They offer phone service, but it must be cell phones as there are no phone lines here, much less power lines. My partner gets out and talks to a woman who works there. She tells her that we are from a church in Tucson and asks if we can park and give water, food, socks, and tennis shoes to those migrants who need it. The woman says fine. She says over the course of the evening until the morning there will be three to four hundred migrants dropped off here. She tells us to park in the shade of a scraggly mesquite tree.

It is now around 4:30 in the afternoon, and the first visitors are children who live in this strange junkyard of humanity. They are all covered in a sheen of dust the color of the red burnt adobe, and all but one are barefoot. We give them candies. The barefoot kids look longingly at the box of used donated shoes we brought. An older child named Louis Diego climbs on the bed of the truck and sorts through the shoes until he finds a pair that fit him. He asks if he can have them. I ask if he has no shoes, and he tells me he does, but only for school, so we give him the ones he has found. The feet of the other kids are too small to fit any of the shoes we have.

A van comes down the road and parks in front of a house across the way. The driver gets out and opens the rear doors and the side doors. The van has come from Altar with a load of migrants, locked in for the ride. They pour out and start walking toward a truck with a cage over its bed. Soon this group of migrants is again heading down the road, this time in the back of a Ford pickup, standing shoulder to shoulder. I'm told they will ride like this for maybe an hour or so to whatever trailhead their runner is told is open.

Another van comes, and then another. Two small girls exit, along with older adults. One is around eight or nine and the other ten or eleven. Like sisters, I think. They are in the care of a big Mexican with tattoos. They all come over to our truck and look over our supplies. I tell them to take whatever they need. "Tiene mota?" the big Mexican asks. Do you have marijuana? I tell him no, and he and some of the men chuckle.

The girls look for shoes that might fit them and chatter excitedly. There are none small enough for them. The two girls seem eager and enthusiastic, almost as if they are on a camping trip with their uncle and this is part of the sideshow before they go hiking. I know soon enough these two young innocents will be hunkered down in pitch-black dark waiting for the guide to say all clear and that the run across will be without any light except the moon to mark the way. The desert is treacherous. It can be terrifying to an adult, much less children, and these two are entrusted to a guy that wants to get high.

My partner tells me later that someone in the group told her they would be at milepost 7 on Arivaca Road tomorrow at 10:00 in the morning. I am at least relieved that if nothing bad happens they can hike that thirteen miles as the crow flies in one night, and when the sun rises they will be dropping down into a green glade with lots of big shade trees. Maybe that big Mexican will have carried them on his broad back when they got tired and delivered his human cargo to whoever paid to have those little girls safe and sound in their arms.

The group is led over to a pickup truck as another van unloads migrants. We keep passing out supplies. I look up as the truck carrying those two little girls heads down the road. There is a lull in activity, and a pig and two young sucklings nose around the yard. A woman named Anparna introduces herself. She sells ice to the tiendas and tells us that if we ever have to spend the night on this side of the border she would be glad to put us up in her house and tells us where she lives.

A van stops next to our truck and unloads more migrants. After picking through our supplies they get back in the van. The man on the passenger side talks to someone on his cell phone. I go to check the time in the cab of my truck, and one of the migrants hops out of the van and asks if I have a jacket since it will be cold in the night and all he has is a tank-top shirt. For some reason I had brought along a short-sleeve dress shirt that I really liked. Now it went on the back of a migrant stealing his way across the border in style—my style, anyway.

We are running out of supplies and time, as the port of entry closes at 8:00 p.m. It will take a while to get back to the border on the bumpy road. The vans will keep coming late into the night, but we must go or we will be spending the night at our new friend Anparna's house. We drop what supplies we do have left at her house on the way back, and she tells us she will distribute them to migrants.

It is seven thirty when we stop at a taco stand in the center of Sasabe. We are five minutes from the gate that separates my country from Mexico, but it seems much further. As the light begins to fade, the town is coming alive. We hear the sound of clattering hoofs, and a young man canters up to the taco stand on a Mexican pony and greets the young girl who prepared our food. As they talk, the señora of the house keeps an eye on the couple as she watches a soap opera on the television.

It is time to go. In five minutes we are at the gate and into the United States.

The highway is wet from fresh downpours, and as we chase the northward-moving storms the lightning on the horizon is frenetic and frequent. The desert gives up its earthy creosote smell. In the headlights I watch my truck run over two snakes and a toad in the forty-three miles to Three Points. I think of the two little girls and their journey this night, and I pray for a safe and gentle crossing.

Story Sixteen

We drive south into Mexico in a two-car caravan, my truck loaded with shoes and socks, gallons of hydrogen peroxide, bandages, foot cream, baby formula, a scale, and pregnancy test kits, the other car loaded with a doctor, a nurse, a photographer, and a translator.

The trip had been planned and then postponed a couple of times, and the medical supplies had been stacked in my living room for a couple of months. We are going to Altar, a small village about fifty miles south of the border and a staging area for migrants who will be crossing into the United States. At any one time there are between five hundred and a thousand migrants from all over Mexico and Central America in this town.

Our mission is to go to a shelter where we will set up a clinic and drop off supplies. The shelter is a for-profit venture, and I am told the migrants pay a dollar a day for lodging and two meals.

The trip down is beautiful and uneventful. As we near the town I notice a new Pemex gas station. There are some older-model vans filled with human cargo purchasing gas. The station sits incongruously in the middle of nowhere, servicing the tremendous amount of traffic on the dirt road to our right. Our guide tells me to turn right onto this dirt road where a toll booth with a chain blocks the way. We park and watch as a van approaches the booth and stops. Money is exchanged, the chain drops, and the van continues north. I am told the toll is two dollars per car and three dollars a van. The road goes to the brickyard in Sasabe. The road used to be free, but an enterprising entrepreneur bought the road, or at least this junction, and is taking advantage of the traffic to make a living.

We continue east on the paved highway for five miles and arrive in Altar. Here the last leg of the migrants' journey in Mexico is nearly over.

Soon they will be in the United States. Buses from all over Mexico arrive and disgorge migrants in Altar's main plaza. The plaza is surrounded by open-air stalls in which is sold everything a migrant will need for a desert crossing: backpacks, hats, plastic bags, toiletries, shoes, all of the things we have found discarded out in the desert on the U.S. side. There is a brand-new bank on the corner and a couple of other money-changing houses where wire transfers can be made. Little groups of migrants congregate in the sparse shade waiting for contacts to lead them to a place to stay the night, and the payphones are surrounded by young men with concerned and weary faces watching the speaker talk with family.

We stop at a corner store, our destination. Here a woman has a small tortilla factory behind a counter. The front of the store is stocked with some dry goods. Behind the counter she sits, counting pesos a young man with dyed blonde hair has spread before her. I will later see him cruising the plaza. This woman runs a shelter for migrants. She provides them with a place to stay and two meals a day that consist mainly of rice and beans with tortillas and the occasional egg. We are all introduced to her, and then we bring in the supplies. The woman then leads us through a doorway into a small courtyard, surrounded by the rooms she rents. The rooms are of two types. The upper ones appear to be a little nicer, since they have doors. The ones below do not even have that. They all have bunks made of iron with plywood beds covered only with a piece of carpet. There is not one other stick of furniture in any of the rooms. There are three very clean bathrooms, two of them containing a shower, and there is a sink for washing clothes in the little courtyard.

The owner calls out to the migrants and introduces us, and then our guide goes upstairs and announces herself to the men upstairs. She rousts them all, telling them to come down to receive information, medical care, and supplies for their journey.

There are fifty of them in all, including a few women and a young girl. Our guide gives a long speech, warning them of the dangers of their endeavor and letting them know what we will be doing. They all look tired. Some have looks of desperation and despair, others of resignation, and still others look to be in good spirits considering their situation. By a show of hands, many have been deported once already, and some twice.

The men on the balcony above have not crossed yet. They are different from the group below. They are not as small in stature as the group in the courtyard, and for the most part their skin is lighter in color. One of these men listens intently and asks our guide political questions about the policies of the U.S. government.

Our guide finishes her talk. Then we check the migrants' feet for blisters while our guide rounds up the women to give them pregnancy tests and our doctor attempts to find out the symptoms of a young man who says he is ill. He has tried to cross twice and been caught each time; the second time he was separated from his medicine, which he uses to control his epilepsy. He shows us the prescription, and the doctor recognizes only one of the drug names.

The doctor is having trouble understanding what his symptoms are. Our guide who is fluent in Spanish is busy with the women, so the young man's condition is not attended to at this time. Later we will be sure to check on him.

We have the migrants soak their feet in a water and hydrogen peroxide solution, and then the doctor and the nurse look them over, bandaging blisters. All are given socks and shoes, and some take hats. We give them cans of liquid food, while our guide informs us that all of the women have tested negative for pregnancy.

The doctor goes back to attend to the young epileptic in a quiet corner. He takes his blood pressure and hears his story as told through our guide. On his second attempt to cross he had a seizure when the Border Patrol chased his group. He was separated from his backpack that contained his medicine, and when the Border Patrol detained him they gave him no treatment. This was three days ago. He had no money to buy the medicine and was going to try crossing the border on Friday, just two days away. The doctor tells him he needs to wait at least a week before trying again, and the young man and I go off to purchase his medicine at a pharmacy.

When I return we say our good-byes and go to the plaza. There stands a Red Cross trailer, staffed by a single man who has been passing out Gatorade in dry packets to migrants on and off during the day. He is napping when we go by.

On the drive back our guide reports that the people of Altar were worried about business. It was way down over the last few months. Rumors were that the Mexican government had put up a checkpoint in Hermosillo, Sonora, and was pulling people off the buses before they reached Altar. It was thought the U.S. government was directly supporting this checkpoint with supplies and money.

The residents of Altar have been making a living off the "fenómeno inmigrante" for the last ten years. It started as a trickle and then became a flood. Altar became the temporary home to over a thousand migrants a day. The resident population responded with typical entrepreneurial skills. Additions were added to homes to house them, minivans were converted so they could carry thirty people at a time to Sasabe over *la brecha*, and open-air stalls were erected to sell supplies the migrants would need for the crossing.

It is a big business, this business of the movement of thousands of people. The residents of Altar had responded, as market forces tend to shape what happens in a community.

Now it appears to be drying up overnight. How could this be? The answer to this question will be discovered over time. The people will continue to come, if not through Altar then another border town.

The economic forces that draw people are still in full effect. A checkpoint in Hermosillo will not stop them. A roof over their heads and a full belly, with the opportunity to grow and prosper in their own country, will stem the tide. And then the "fenómeno inmigrante" will begin to perhaps flow the other way.

A volunteer provides aid to migrants in the field.

Story Seventeen

I received a call last night from the person who schedules our daily patrols. A young man has lost his brother out in the desert fifty miles west of Tucson and is worried sick about it. He has been separated from family. Our job will be to try and find him in the great stretch of desert west of the Baboquivari Mountains. It will be next to impossible, but we shall see what we can do.

Today is a day of "making merit." In Thailand, the most common form of honoring this Buddhist doctrine is to offer food to monks when they make their early-morning rounds. The gift is amplified according to the level of the person with whom one makes merit. This "amplification" will increase good karma—but the recipient, not the donor, is the amplifier. What this means is that if I offer food to a thief or a robber, not nearly as much good karma will befall me as if I had offered the food to a saint.

I arrive at the church and a young woman is there. I don't know her. My partner is last week's young traveler, the one I had gone on patrol with. She is heading out alone in her personal car to look for the long-lost brother and gives us specific directions when we get to the area in the desert where she thinks he may be. "You go north," she says, "and I'll head south."

We are heading out to the Tohono O'odham Nation today. I've gone out there only once. The rules are different. You must stay on paved roads and cannot cross the barbed wire that stretches endlessly on either side of the road. The tribe will not allow Humane Borders to put water stations on their land. The number of migrants who die crossing the reservation is higher than in any other area.

The Nation, with its huge swaths of uninhabited desert, draws large numbers of migrants all the same. The Tohono O'odham land stretches north from the border of Mexico nearly seventy-five miles at its widest and is more than one hundred miles long. Out in that desolate desert, the chances of being spotted by the Border Patrol decrease dramatically. So do a person's chances of survival.

My cell phone rings. It is another group of Samaritans out of Green Valley. They have been ordered out to the reservation as well and don't really know who they are looking for and what they are to do with him if they find him. I tell them to look for a migrant in a red hat with a mustache named José Meneses. That is all the information I have.

The man we are looking for was with a group of seventy who crossed on the west side of the Baboquivaris, walked for three nights, and then got separated. There is nothing north of the border on the west side of this range for many miles until you get to Route 86 apart from a couple of small Indian villages. Once people get to the highway, they have to wait for a ride on a road that is crawling with Border Patrol or continue north for another fifty miles of desert to Interstate 8.

Four miles west of Three Points, and with the cold of morning at its greatest, we see four people on the side of the road. They are a family, two brothers and a sister, along with the wife of the youngest brother. The sister is a jovial woman even in these circumstances, and she has a bright smile with lots of silver teeth. The wife has wrenched her knee pretty badly and cannot walk any longer. Her shoes are off as well, and that tells me she has blisters. We help her into the back seat of the truck and I gingerly pull off her socks. The left foot has a large blister on the big toe and the heel. The right foot has a large blister on the heel. None of the blisters have broken yet, so we give her clean socks. Her left knee is giving her a lot of pain, and she cannot put much weight on it. It is first light and very cold, so we get all four in the truck and keep it running with the heater on full blast.

They are from Chiapas. They want to go back to Mexico, so my young companion calls Border Patrol. The older brother asks how far it is to Tijuana from Nogales by bus. I figure they will try to cross there next. While we wait for the Border Patrol, I offer them food. They are grateful and hungry. The sister pops open a can of Vienna sausage, and they all dig in except for the wife, who seems depressed and in pain.

They had started out thirty-two strong from Mexico and had been moving at a good clip to reach Route 86 in two days and three nights. On the third night, though, she had taken a bad fall. Once the young woman was injured she could not keep up, and the coyote told them he was leaving them by the road. The rest of the group continued north.

The Border Patrol agent arrives and is a big towhead with an Okie accent and a nice smile. I start in right off.

"We found them on the side of the road. They want to go back and this one has a knee that is injured pretty bad. She can hardly walk. They are all family. Two brothers and a sister. The one who is injured is married to the younger brother. I know you guys will take them to Tucson, but will she get medical care? I hope you don't split them up."

"Uh huh, yeah they'll go to Tucson and we have someone will give her a look. We heard the sheriff called this in. Was it you all?"

My young companion says, "I don't know. I just called it in about a half hour ago."

"Yeah, well, we're getting so many calls right now dispatch can't keep up."

And then the good-byes. I shake the older brother's hand, "Buena suerte," and then the younger brother and his wife. Finally the sister, Maria Anita, who when I grab her hand to shake it kisses me on each cheek as warmly and gratefully as if she were walking out the door of a restaurant I once owned having sat down to a steak, not Vienna sausages out of a can. My last image of the group is a white SUV, unmarked, that arrives on the scene. The man who gets out scowls at us as we drive away.

We head west and find the road we are to go north on. We do so. We run across the young woman who told us to go north, and she says the south part of the road played out after a half a mile. There's plenty of migrant trash here, but no José with a red cap and a mustache. When we get back to 86, we decide to head west for about ten miles, and then turn around and check every culvert and turnout back to Tucson.

Our satellite phone rings and the call is from command central, asking us to redirect our mission. There is a report of four migrants in need off a dirt road past San Luis, which looks to be about seventy-five miles away on Indian Route 15 near milepost 40.

"We'll never find them," my companion says.

I disregard his comments. "Let's do it."

In Sells we see the third dead dog on the road since we left Tucson two and a half hours ago, all fresh kills and all in the westbound lanes.

We stop at a gas station and get directions to the highway where the migrants are supposed to be. We jam it, and as we fly along I begin to wonder if we are being sent on a wild-goose chase and if my young companion is correct.

Route 15 is a good paved highway, so we drive fast. We see maybe five cars in the thirty-five minutes it takes to get up to milepost 40.

Every so often we see a road sign with an arrow pointing down a dirt road to villages with names like Kohatk, Sif Vaya, and Chuichu.

Just past milepost 40, big power lines intersect Route 15. A dirt road to access the big towers heads off in either direction. We slow way down and look in both directions. The road to the west is completely exposed for a long way. To the east it has a little more cover, but not much. The migrants, I'm guessing, would have kept on walking.

We are at a standstill in the road assessing the situation when I see a white SUV heading south in front of us about two miles up the road. As it gets closer, we can tell that it's some kind of law enforcement vehicle, with a uniformed driver and a cage between him and the rear passenger seats. He checks us out as we check him out.

We head back south, and as we do we see three white vehicles come around the bend, heading north at a good clip. My young companion trains the field glasses on them. "Border Patrol," he says.

"Are they following us? Do they know why we are here?"

They zip by us at seventy miles an hour. I wait for a bit, then make a right turn onto the dirt road and ease in and out of a gully and head east slowly. The power lines are making a crackling noise as we slowly move down the road. We go three hundred yards, and then I spot the four people lying down behind some small creosote bushes. They wake as we approach and look alarmed. We shout out the Samaritan greeting in Spanish.

I drive past them and look for a place to park the truck. There is no place at all. Creosote brush is the only thing around. We are visible from the highway for anyone who might be taking the time to look.

There are two women and two men. I walk up and crouch on my knees in front of the four. They are standing now in front of me and are barely taller than my crouching position. They are beautiful little people from some strange land with perfect proportions and dark eyes that seem tired but resolute. Their ages are incalculable. The men are strong, the two women tired but ready to continue when nightfall cloaks them for the walk. They have journeyed far.

They have no water or food left; so it is good we have found them. They do not want to give up. One woman has her shoes off and has two large blisters on her heels. I ask where they are from, and she says Guatemala. I ask how long they have been walking, and she says two weeks. They are approximately eighty miles from the Mexican border on a straight line. My young companion is off-loading food and water, socks and gloves when I look up and see the Border Patrol car coming down the highway, heading north.

It zooms by.

They want to know how far it is to Casa Grande. Sixteen kilometers, I tell them. The women look disappointed at the distance. The men not fazed. They have journeyed almost three thousand kilometers from Guatemala, so sixteen kilometers is nothing much.

I go back to the truck to get the medical bag so I can try and bandage the blisters and look north up the road. Some cars are stopped at the crest of the hill, and something is going on. I grab the field glasses and train them on three Border Patrol cars with lights flashing, blocking the road. We have been spotted for sure. And now we need to get out of there, as my greatest fear is to cause the arrest of those who do not wish to come in.

We throw packs of food at their feet and scores of water bottles, hop in the truck, and head out to the pavement. We can't drive fast as the dirt road is rough, and we can't see the crest of the hill where the Border Patrol is parked because of the creosote lining the road.

It takes one minute for us to reach the pavement, and my heart is thumping. We look north and find the road empty. We are dumbfounded. No Border Patrol. They are gone. My young companion looks through the field glasses and confirms this. We head north at patrol speed, forty miles an hour. What happened? Where are they? Why the flashing lights? Are they hiding from us? What is going on? I briefly consider going back to the Guatemaltecos but decide against it, since the white Ford SUV has reappeared and is now about two miles behind us. We slow down to see if he pulls into the dirt utility road at milepost 40, but he continues past it. We speed up to get out of there and continue on our way. It is enough merit for one day.

Kathryn

EAST
BOUND..
9.03

Photograph by Kathryn Ferguson

Previous page: Man rides freight train north.

Story Eighteen

Blessed are the gentle.
Blessed are the raucous.
Blessed are the ones who walk.
Blessed are the guides—the moon, the stars, the sacred mountain.
Blessed are the resting places—the shadows, the roots, the rocks,
    the arroyos.
Blessed are the ones who laugh.
Blessed are the ones who dream.
Blessed is the night train.

All strangers, they began the journey down the rabbit hole where night becomes day. They would travel in darkness at night and stop to rest amid the rattlesnakes in sunlight. Only two nights and a day, assured the tall *pollero*, the guide (literally "chicken wrangler"). We've gone this way many times.

There were four polleros. The tall one was thirty years old, the others in their midtwenties. The twenty-four people crossing included four young women; the rest were men between twenty-two and fifty years old. The group had left the lights of Nogales half an hour earlier and was passing through the darkness along the cemetery wall. Sal already felt the heaviness of the backpack, adjusting the straps of the *mochila* to lessen the pain on his shoulder.

He made the sign of the cross again as they passed the high wrought-iron entrance to the dead. I'm glad I'm not alone, he thought. There was no moon, just the smell of dampness in the air. The polleros ordered them not to speak, but his footsteps slapped the ground in unison with the others. That is why he heard so clearly when the man jumped the fence and landed with a heavy smack on the road in front of them. The bandit, purple and brown bandana tied around his face, jerked the pistol side to side, pointing it quickly at the two polleros in front, then at Sal. The woman behind Sal screamed, and the second thief ran up to the rear of the line, which was flanked by the other two polleros. The thief pushed the polleros forward, causing two men to fall, then the next two fell like dominos. And the chaos began.

The thieves worked quickly, ripping necklaces off the women, ordering everyone to throw cash, watches, jewelry into burlap bags. The thief with the long carving knife ordered two young brothers to remove their shoes. They were expensive black and silver tennis shoes of the highest style, never worn before. Along with the brothers' other belongings and the three thousand dollar crossing fee, all the families in the brothers' small pueblo in Michoacán had chipped in to buy the shoes. Families had organized for weeks, pooling money and property, preparing for the brothers' long dark journey. They were the hope of the town. The entire pueblo stayed up all night with the family, waiting for dawn to send the young men off. Everyone talked and cried as if it were a funeral, sending the boys *al otro lado*, to the other side. And now in five minutes, the shoes were gone, and so were the thieves.

The women stopped crying, and the polleros quieted everyone. The problem was clear. Everyone was grave. They all understood the enormity of the theft. A man cannot walk the desert without shoes and live. The appointed time for the journey had come, and there would be no returning to Nogales to look for shoes. A couple of compadres gave them socks so the brothers had three socks on each foot.

Moving into even more intense darkness, weighted down with dread, the travelers began again. Sal was joined by a fear that was never to leave him. He knew he wouldn't make it.

They left behind the last lights of civilization and began climbing silently into the small hills, no flashlights to guide the way. Sal was already bone-tired traveling from his home in Acapulco to Nogales. The previous night he had been in a hotel full of immigrants, lying on the floor in a room with no furniture. Lying next to strangers, he couldn't sleep. All this day he was tired and nervously waited for night to begin the journey. He was grateful as the terrain changed to a flat plain. Clouds hid the moon; so it was hard to see even the young woman in front of him. At least there was a little breeze.

He thought of his enchanting five-year-old girl, who wouldn't let go of him when he got in the truck to leave his barrio. She would always say, "I love you, Apa, you are the best." He thought of her round face and shiny black hair. She was not of his blood, but she was his daughter.

Migrants pass this image painted on a hillside near the border at Nogales, Sonora.

He loved his four grown-up children, but this one was special. Maybe because she might be the last. He was forty-four and diabetic. "I am old," he thought. "Forty-four is not old, but with diabetes it is. Who knows what will happen?" As he stumbled on a rock, his thoughts of her were like a walking stick, guiding him among the stones.

After a few hours, the group stopped to rest. The damp night air felt good. It was good to sit. The four polleros sat with them. Sal had been afraid of them at first; he thought them ugly and dirty. But it occurred to him that in a few hours he and his companions would be as dusty as they were. The guide with the pockmarked face explained how to ration the food and water. "Be especially careful of the water," he said. "Only a little at a time when we stop, and never drink while we walk." He reminded them to walk fast while the night was new. They picked up their packs to move on. Their trail paralleled the border, climbing into steeper and steeper hills, all edges sharp now. They inched their way down a steep trail made of small broken rocks, sliding more than walking. Sal could see no faces, only a line of shadowy bent forms maneuvering the slope. Below was darkness.

The last migrant jumped down from the canyon trail and hit the flat arroyo floor where moonlight shot down from the clouds onto glittery sand. Sal was greatly relieved to be able to see again with the bright moon. The narrow arroyo was flanked by high cliffs, and walking was easier. The only sounds he heard were the clicks of night insects.

The group rounded a bend onto a wide flat area of smooth sand lined by tall trees and thick bushes. Sal, walking in the middle of the tired group, was watching his feet to see where he stepped and suddenly bumped into a woman who had abruptly stopped in front of him. He looked up and couldn't believe what he was seeing. In the middle of the wash stood two skinny *cholos* who could have just stepped off the metro in Mexico City. They wore bandanas tied around their foreheads, earrings, and black rayon Megadeth T-shirts hanging to their knees. Wide bracelets and gold chains hanging down their chests shone like gold of an Aztec emperor. In the center of the light sand, they were set in bas-relief, lit by a spotlight of white moonlight against the black cliffs.

Ceremoniously lifting rigid arms, pistol in a two-handed grip, the red-eyed cholo pointed a gun directly into the face of the guide, shouting, "Stop!" His companion giggled "Bienvenidos a la playa!" Welcome to the beach. Herding the rest of Sal's companions from the rear, a rancid cholo with a gleaming stiletto pushed the straggled group together.

The two wired cholos moved fast. The one with the silver front tooth stood quietly to the side, his gun aimed at the group. The *vato* with the ponytail and glassy eyes shouted at everyone to throw down money and jewelry. The tall pollero yelled, "¡Oye, pendejo, déjalos en paz! ¡Ya les robaron . . . ya no tienen nada!" "Listen, asshole, leave 'em alone! They've already been robbed . . . they have nothing!" The red-eyed cholo adjusted his bandana and ordered two older migrants to take off their pants, knowing that money is often sewn inside secret pockets. They refused. The bandit ground his teeth and slugged one man in the face; the other bandit hit the second migrant with the butt of his gun. A woman screamed, and other migrants helped the men regain balance. The bandits took the men's pants and, finding no money, threw them toward the bushes.

All the while, Silver Tooth stood quietly, his gun pointed at the group. Sal saw the bandit move slowly toward him with the cool focus of a rattlesnake. Like lightning, the bandit reached out his arm and grabbed the young girl next to Sal. The man put the gun in his waist and tore the girl's shirt, pulling her forward by both breasts. She screamed and snapped her head away from him. "¡Cállate!" "Shut up!" he yelled. He grabbed her arm, rapidly dragging her toward the trees. She whispered, "Help me," and started crying. The tall guide shouted "¡Déjala!" "Leave her alone!" The other two *bajadores*, lowlifes, moved toward the pollero, guns aimed. He shouted, "If you hurt her, we will kill you." The *pistolero* said, "We're armed; you have nothing." The pollero said, "Maybe you will shoot a couple of us, but there are twenty-eight of us and only three of you; so we will kill you." The cholo considered this. He shouted to his friend, "Leave her alone. Let's go." The bandits grabbed as many gallons of water as they could carry and ran up the trail on the other side of the canyon wall. They were gone. Sal was shaken. I want to go back, he thought. One young man vomited. The women gathered around the young girl, who was sobbing. One pollero told everyone to drink water. One pollero walked to the girl and touched her arm. He said, "Let's keep walking."

Sal didn't know anyone's name. He felt lonely. We help each other, but we are strangers, he thought. The group slowly began walking up the wash. It was one in the morning. It had been only five hours since the first robbery.

As they walked in the night, Sal wrestled with the notion of going home. His throat was parched, not from lack of water but from fear. Could he turn around, leave everyone here, and find his way back? He would be lost in a heartbeat. And surely something terrible would happen if he ran into the *asaltantes*, assailants, with no group to ward them off. But the most chilling thought of all was that there was nothing to go back to. The *colonia*, neighborhood, in Acapulco, oh what problems. An American friend once said, "Acapulco, what a great place to live, the beaches, the sea." For you, Sal had gently told the American. "At home I earn one U.S. dollar an hour. And one chicken costs fifty pesos, five dollars." No, no he thought, I cannot go home to the five-dollar chicken.

Sal's calf muscles were cramping. He carefully carved all thoughts of pain out of his mind. He carefully replaced them with thoughts of his arrival in New York. Benny, the owner of the Italian Garden, had said, "Sal, you will always have a job here." Sal had worked there for four years. He started as a busboy but preferred to prepare the beautiful plates of food rather than clean them. He liked how the hot sea bass was placed gently on top of the fine pasta, and how the chef ladled the halved red grapes cooked in wine and butter sauce over the fish. He liked that the salad had purple leaves in it.

Once, at two in the morning, when the kitchen was being cleaned, Sal created a small masterpiece and took it to Benny, who was at the cash register. One bite into the dish, Benny promoted Sal to a kitchen assistant.

Initially, Sal had worked eighty hours a week as a busboy. He earned $4 per hour plus tips, $700 per week. But they removed $250 in taxes, mostly for social security, from each check. Money he would never see. I don't understand why the president doesn't want us to come to his country, and why we travel here like animals, he had thought. Sal did the math again as he had so many times before. Multiply $250 by thousands and thousands and thousands of migrants. That would buy a couple of chickens, he thought.

No one had spoken for hours. Sal wondered when they could sleep. At least they were on level ground again, running. The night train moved on.

Not far away, Sal saw something moving toward them. Swaying and bobbing, it moved closer. Clop clop clop. Shifting and reeling, tall like a centaur with no head. It slowly approached but moved with no malice. Then Sal could see. It was not one but six. Four burros and two men. One scruffy man walked in front, then a young man, stoop-shouldered, flanked the four burros packed high with layers of fat burlap bags. Two bags side by side covered with two more until there was a pyramid of seven bags. *Mota.* Marijuana. Men and burros moved steadily and patiently, giving no notice of the twenty-eight travelers they were about to encounter. One man with a burro carried a *cuerno de chivo*, goat's horn (an AK-47). The pollero leading the group silently flicked his hand back, motioning them to step off the road. No one spoke as the procession passed, with neither burros nor men acknowledging Sal and his companions. Silently, the migrants moved on.

Just before dawn, walking along a small dirt road, the migrants could hear cattle in the distance. The polleros pushed them on, wanting to cover a few more miles before they would rest. They came upon a woman and her mother, walking the same direction as the group.

"¿Como le va?" "How's it going?" the woman asked.

"Bien," said the pollero.

"¿Van al otro lado?" "Are you going to the States?"

"Yes."

"Can we go with you?"

"No."

"Why not? We need to be with other people."

"You'll never make it."

That's when Sal saw the other woman's eyes. In the dark, he could see that her world was darker. Her eyes were open, but she saw nothing.

"Please, let us come with you. My daughter is in Oregon."

"She can't go," the pollero said, pointing to the older woman. "A blind woman can't travel where we are going. Go back. The path gets ugly."

"Can we walk with you just a little while, no more? We have no men with us."

"Okay, but in a few kilometers we leave you. Soldiers patrol here. Maybe they'll help."

She nodded. Everyone moved fast, including the blind grandmother. At a fork in the road, the group stopped. They were still in Mexico but could almost touch the line. Not far away, they could see lights from a Mexican ranch house. The pollero told the two women, "This is where you stay. Sit and wait."

"Please, just a little more," said the woman.

"No, this is your last chance to stay alive. From now on it will be impossible for you."

As the pollero placed a gallon of water and a bundle of food on a rock for the woman, Sal decided to stay, too. He was scared. It was his last chance to go home. He had heard about terrible deaths on the desert. He didn't want to die. He had a big white house, eight hundred square feet where he lived with his five children and his mother. When he was a boy, it had been two hundred square feet.

He had lived his entire life in one room until the last fifteen years, when he slowly acquired materials to add to his house. Now he had three bedrooms, an indoor kitchen, and a center room. Outside by the front door was a huge gnarled bougainvillea covered in cherry-red flowers. Next to that was a small garden with roses and coconut palms. Yes, thought Sal, I want to go home.

But then he saw his mother in the house sitting with two grandchildren on her lap, playing with her long gray hair. She sat by the Virgin of Guadalupe altar. She was happy and laughing with the kids, touching them more because she saw less. She was diabetic and could see very little now, like this old woman on the road.

Sal's family had no food, and his mother had lost so much weight that her dresses engulfed her. She looked like a little girl in grown-up clothes.

And Sal remembered the wood crucifix hanging above the door and how his Jesus had suffered and how what he himself was experiencing was nothing compared to the horror of the crucifixion, and how even though the bougainvillea was red and healthy his family was not, and he couldn't permit himself to think of returning with nothing, so he had to go on with the group, climb back on the train.

Fingers of apricot light lay on the horizon. They left the two women on the road, left the night behind, and searched for big trees to rest under.

Beneath the mesquites, they ate a little. Some talked, some slept. They rested there most of the day. Water was almost gone. Away from the migrants, the polleros lay on the ground, talking. Sal heard the thirty-year-old say he had been in prison for five years. "What for?" his friend asked. "I couldn't pay the *pinche* cop. He wanted more. I didn't have no more money. He put me away. But God likes me; he gave me this tour guide job. It's a good job. Do two trips a week for a few months, take some time off."

In the afternoon, slightly rested, the group moved on. Soon it was dark. The stars reminded Sal of the hundreds of burning candlewicks at the cathedral altar. He wondered was one lit for him. He wondered was one lit for the cholo who tried to rape the girl back in the arroyo. He wondered who would light a candle for such a man, but he imagined someone might. A better person than he was, he thought.

In the night, the migrants stepped across a barbed-wire fence into the United States. Just before the first light of day they rested. Two polleros scouted ahead, disappearing over a rise. Half an hour later they returned, worried. The hills were covered with National Guard troops sitting under camouflage tents.

The polleros argued a while. Normally, they would have continued here on this trail. Now they had to detour into unknown territory, away from the soldiers. Leaving the trail, they gathered the group, bush-whacking west.

They saw the first helicopters. For the rest of the journey, they would hide from them in the mornings and afternoons. The woman walking next to Sal was frightened. She was told that they shoot migrants from the helicopter.

As they walked the ridge of the hills, Sal began to worry. They were heading into deep canyons. He was tired and had no more water.

Slipping down a steep bank into an arroyo, all twenty-eight travelers rejoiced. A living stream. Sal scrambled to the edge, throwing water into his mouth from cupped hands. He filled his empty gallon jug and a smaller bottle.

The group moved into a narrow of high, slick rock walls. Directly ahead was another wall, three houses high. They were in a box canyon. The polleros argued. Sal was afraid. His fear increased as he realized the polleros were also afraid. They had seen no trail all day, the sun would be down soon.

Backtracking, one pollero pointed to a canyon wall five hundred meters high. There was an animal trail at the base, going up, then out of sight. "This way," said the pollero. Looking up, Sal thought, I can't do it. Some of the migrants refused to go. "You have to!" yelled the pollero. "We have no other choice!" Everyone secured backpacks. The two young men with no shoes asked for more socks. They started up the trail. As dark clouds rolled over the sky above, they began to climb, two polleros in front, two behind. Within the first few steps, Sal's heart raced. The path was so steep he had to pitch his body forward to maintain balance.

As he lifted his foot to step onto the next rock, his thigh screamed. Dehydration was affecting his muscles. One step, he thought. One more step.

It got darker. They could hear the rain before they could see it. Then it began to spit. The line of travelers slowly inched up the switch-backs. There came a crack of thunder and lightning. The group spread out, looking for shelter, pressing against scraggly bushes near the cliff wall. Sal and a woman moved under a narrow rock overhang. The rain hit the ground and bounced back up soaking their feet and legs. Keep going, yelled the pollero below. They moved on.

Sal heard rocks falling. Someone screamed. Sal looked down. A forty-year-old man had fallen. He tumbled and slid down fifteen feet past the two last men onto the trail below. One of the guides went to help him. "Keep going!" shouted the other. After the pollero helped the man, they resumed climbing.

It was steep now. The nearly invisible trail went straight up a narrow crevice. Sal had to climb hand over hand. He placed his fingers on a slippery rock above, putting his foot on a stone below, pushing himself up. His lungs burned. This seemed to go on forever. He was drenched in rain and sweat.

They reached the top, a flat mesa. They sat down, rain pouring off their heads like cattle in the field. They slept in the wet dirt.

The next day, from the mesa top, the polleros could see for miles. Below, they could see a ranch they recognized. The travelers passed down out of the canyons onto the desert, heading for the ranch road. One girl fell behind, ill. She hadn't eaten for two days and could not keep up. A pollero gave her crackers and waited until she could continue.

The group passed through the hot August sun looking for a place to rest. There was no shade, only cholla cactus as far as the eye could see. They stopped to rest in the sun. Even the guides were exhausted. Sal looked at each face and saw sadness. We are connected by grief, he thought.

Instead of a two-night journey, they were now in their fifth afternoon. The polleros said they would never go that route again. It was terrible, they said. On Interstate 19, fifteen miles from Nogales, there is a permanent Border Patrol checkpoint. The guides said they usually take the migrants on a day's walk around the checkpoint. Because of the National Guard presence, they changed their plans.

Now they waited. All afternoon, they had walked in the shade of big trees near a small wash, along a gas pipeline. It was seven in the evening. Sal felt sick and hungry. He was waiting with four women and one man. His was the last group. Three rides had come for the others. They were waiting in groups of six for their polleros to come back with a car, pick them up, and take them to Phoenix, three hours away.

Suddenly Sal looked up. He couldn't believe it. His ride was here. They saw the car turn around and pull over to where they stood by the side of the road. Everyone piled in. As Sal jumped in and shut the door, they saw a Border Patrol vehicle make a fast U-turn, coming up behind them. The pollero drove fast to the bridge. He hit his brakes, slamming hard into the small wall of the bridge. The door flew open and Sal flew out, hitting his chest and left shoulder on the pavement. The pollero yelled "Follow me!" They ran under the bridge into some trees.

After twenty minutes, Sal couldn't keep up. The pain was searing. He couldn't take one more step. His collarbone was broken. He couldn't move an inch to the right or left without immense pain. Even a single step was debilitating. He lay under a tree in the dirt. He was finished. He had eaten two cans of tuna and one bag of chips in five days. No water for two days. He was lost, alone. He couldn't move. "God, I know you took me from the others. Whatever you want, I will do what you ask. I am finally listening." And he gave himself up to his god.

Two hours later, he managed to stand. He saw lights near a road. There was a parking area and a soda machine. Nearby, two policemen were talking by their cars. He walked up to them. "I'm hurt," he said. "Do you have water?" They looked at him, gave him water, asked for his ID. He showed them his Mexican driver's license. They looked him over, called an ambulance, waited with him. When they put him in the ambulance headed for a Tucson hospital, one said, "You're gonna be okay, man."

My friend, Helen, a nurse, brought a chair for me. The three of us sat close. Slanted rays of light from the tall window reflected back from the shiny floor. Pockets of darkness lay in the corners. Sal was a quiet religious man. He spoke softly. We had to lean forward to hear. Sal spoke of his god and gifts and promises. He said he had never endured such a journey before, and said that he would try to be a better man. At the end of the long tale, Sal talked about his mother. He began to cry softly, then harder. He cried until his torso shook. We cried with him.

What part of man can endure torture and grief and not be changed by it, Sal asked. Maybe that is the real gift given to man, he said. That under any horrific circumstance for any length of time, right up to the moment of leaving life, one part of us remains intact. Maybe that is what the soul is, he said. I am still alive, I am blessed, he whispered.

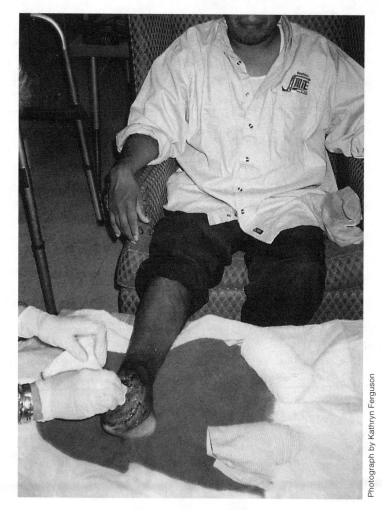

Treatment of Carlos's amputated foot.

Story Nineteen

Kachung! He heard the sound long before he felt anything. He was gripping a bar at the back of the railcar, hanging on the outside with his feet propped against the base of the car. Shielding himself from the November night wind, he tucked his head down and didn't see what was happening.

The train braked hard at a siding to allow another train to pass. The railcar behind Carlos jerked forward and hit his car, forcing his foot up and under the car he was riding. The top half of his foot snapped back at a right angle, the way you would break a stick for kindling. Moments later, the car behind him ricocheted out, freeing his foot. In the clanging, crunching, grinding metal screeches, no one heard his scream as his foot flopped back into normal position as if nothing had happened.

He froze. Everything stopped. He couldn't remember how to breathe. He couldn't see. Thoughts slowly moved across his mind. He should ungrip his fingers from the bar. He should look around for the *migra*. He should look at his foot. He should move. He should hop off the train. He should touch his foot. He should go look for his friends. He should hurry.

"¡Carlos, apúrate!"

Someone whispered his name, urging him to hurry. Carlos was in the dirt on one knee. He couldn't understand what he was supposed to do.

"Get up. Let's go! They'll see us! What's wrong with you?" A companion pulled him up. Another was running ahead, barely visible in dark clothes on a moonless night.

He tried to run with them, to hop onto another railcar they could ride into Tucson. Tears ran down his cheeks, washing the dust off his face. If he put weight on the heel, it lifted the front of the foot, causing such pain that he almost vomited.

"I can't. Go ahead. My foot got smashed. Go on." The men stopped and looked down at the foot. No one said anything. He could hear the wind. Tree leaves moved. Ahead up on the tracks, he could hear men speaking English. He saw a cigarette lighter flick. He was cold.

A few minutes later, hanging on the shoulders of companions, Carlos and the three men moved into deep shadows of the hills, away from the train.

Late the next afternoon, Carlos's traveling companions were restless and anxious. The sun was low on the horizon. They needed to move on, they said. There was a job waiting in Phoenix. Yah, it's okay, Carlos said. I'm fine.

One of the men cleared a space in the dirt near where Carlos sat. They brushed away rocks and twigs. From the backpacks, they took some burritos wrapped in paper and laid them in the clean area. They laid down cans of tuna and sardines, tortillas, a couple of small cans of jalapeños, bags of potato chips, *saladitos*, limes, and packs of crushed cookies. They set down rectangular bottles of Electrolit and two plastic gallon jugs of water. These were all the supplies they had brought with them, enough food for a person for a week. One man laid a wool plaid shirt over a creosote bush so Carlos could grab it and throw it over him in the night when he got cold. The good-byes were short. The train was coming. They had to hurry. Been good traveling with you. Hope your foot won't be much of a problem. See you. *Qué les vayan bien.* And they were gone.

He heard the footsteps die away. He sat still for a long while. Silence. Complete silence. He tried to hear anything. Nothing, not even crickets. He was alone. Darkness was coming. He could barely see the shirt on the bush. He thought he should not let himself think beyond or back. He coughed so he could hear something. He had to kill the silence.

In the distance, he heard the train arriving, a soft pounding sound. Familiar. He took a deep breath. It will all be okay. Moments later the train faded away. He listened. Nothing. Then he heard something. He turned to look. No one. He waited. He heard it again. He looked again, then realized it was him. It was his heart pounding. Loud. There was nothing and no one else. His muscles tensed. He tightened inside. Then with a sudden roar, everything he knew to be himself started pushing from the inside out. It was so loud that his head exploded from within. Blood pulsed. The noise in his head was excruciating. Panic. The sun was down. He couldn't see the shirt. He was alone. Nothing inside, nothing outside. But he had felt this before. He knew how to be alone in the fields. He heard himself take a long slow breath. It's going to be okay. He could do this, it would be okay. As soon as he thought that, the panic flooded in again.

৩৩ ৩৩

The nurse took me in to the room.

"Buenos días. ¿Es usted Carlos?" I asked.

"Sí, soy Carlos," he smiled.

"¿Como se siente?"

"Bien, bien."

"I heard about the accident and your foot."

"Ni modo." It doesn't matter, he shrugged. "Just an accident." His square face didn't register emotion.

Both his legs were stretched out, but one was longer. The short leg ended in a blue ball at the foot. Only this foot was half the length of the other. I assumed there were bandages wrapped underneath, but on top everything was covered in what looked like a blue shower cap, a bootie that doctors wear in the operating room.

"¿Cuantos días ha estado aquí?"

"Dos semanas y cuatro días." Two weeks and four days he'd been there.

I set down the Coke, carne asada burrito, and salsa on the table next to him. Nearby was a four-legged aluminum walker.

"Are you training for the Olympics with that thing?" I asked and pointed at the walker.

He laughed and said, "Why not? There's nothing else to do here, except watch what everyone is doing for Christmas Eve tonight."

He reached over to switch off Telemundo, the Spanish-language channel.

"It's better to be here than to be shot at in a war. That's all they show on TV. Since I've been through this, I've had time to think that others have been through worse. This is only an accident; it happens every day."

"What were you doing on the back of a train?"

"Three guys in Obregón asked if I wanted to go with them to a job in Phoenix. We came over to Nogales. For three nights, we walked on the east side of Nogales—it was up and down cliffs and canyons. We got low on food and water. During the day we hid in the trees. We finally got to the train. Each one of us got on the back of a different car. It was only going to be an hour ride to Tucson."

Once Carlos started talking he wouldn't stop. But he just told me the facts, nothing emotional. Most immigrants talk about their families and God. He never mentioned either. He seemed like a man who lived alone. He was a practical man.

"After you got off the train, how long were you out there?"

"Seven days and seven nights."

"Were you scared?"

"No."

"You're brave. I would have been afraid."

"Of course. You're a woman. Women have a right to be afraid. You could be raped. But for a man, there is nothing to fear."

"Were there animals in the night?"

"Only the four-legged kind. I heard coyotes, but they don't bother you. I'm used to the mountains—I've spent lots of time alone. I was in charge of growing and harvesting and often slept alone in the fields."

⋘◐⋙

The next day, after his companions had left, Carlos sat with his back against the tall rocks. Salmon-tinted granite pillars covered with a sheen of green lichen had surrounded him. He sat high on an outcropping where he could see anyone walking below. The pockmarked pillars had large holes where years of desert rain had eaten away the stone. I could build a house here, he thought. Use this rock as a wall.

He felt safe. A thicket of bare mesquites and tall amber grass hid him from the open desert beneath him. Two ravens flew overhead in silhouette, riding an invisible current. The sky was all one color, no real sunlight, no real darkness. Just a November sky. The moist air carried the smell of creosote and damp weeds.

Curiously, there had been no pain yesterday. But today Carlos felt it. It was as if it had been gathering strength all night waiting to attack at dawn. Although it was only his foot that was injured, the slightest twist of his torso hurt. When he pushed himself up against the rock, he was amazed at the intensity of the pain. He reached for his *mochila*, his pack; he always carried Naprosyn. He swallowed the pills, hoping they would help but knowing they wouldn't. They have to help, he thought. I can't go home empty-handed. I have to work.

On the fourth day, Carlos was out of water. He went looking. He walked on his heel down a narrow dirt road and saw a windmill. At the base was a handle he could open for water. He carried it back in two plastic jugs.

The next day, he saw three men walking. He called out to them. They had come from the train and got off to find water. He pointed the way to the windmill. They brought him water and kept him company for a while. They said they were going to Phoenix. They gave him apples and tortillas. They invited him to come, but he told them he was waiting to get better. They left for the train.

Later in the day, Carlos remembered a newspaper article he had read in Obregón about a year earlier. At the railroad yard in Tucson, the bodies of two decapitated men had been found in a tanker car. It was on the Nogales–Tucson line. There were no doors on the car; the only way in was from the top. They had no identification. No one knew what had happened, but it was thought that the men had been riding on their bellies on top of the speeding rail car and poked their heads up just before the train passed beneath a low bridge.

On the seventh day of waiting, Carlos looked at his foot. It was swollen more than ever, nothing but a ball on top, a ball on the bottom. He knew he had to get back on the train and get to Tucson.

When he arrived at the city, he got off the train just before the bridge. He didn't know anyone, so he asked a passerby where he could find shelter. He hobbled a few miles to a public shelter, but he couldn't stay there without U.S. identification. He slept anywhere he could for many nights. After he ran out of food, he started asking strangers for money. He was embarrassed. I'm just like all these weird people walking around, he thought. It's never been this way before in my life. Finally someone told him there was an abandoned house where he could sleep.

The house was on the south side. There was a roof. Some of the windows had no glass, but it was warmer inside. Someone before him had built a fire on the concrete floor. As he was lying there one night staring into the darkness, he thought that he had wanted to come to the United States but realized that a man leaves a lot behind when he leaves his own land.

For almost three weeks, Carlos hobbled from church to shelter, sometimes receiving food, sometimes not. The churches were either closed in the afternoons or they refused to help. He went to the Salvation Army, but they couldn't help him if he didn't have U.S. identification. What about Mexican ID, he asked? I have identification, I am alive, I am standing here. Can't you help? He was told to go to this clinic or that, but no one would give aid.

After almost four weeks, he was very ill. His foot was dark and infected. He had lost fifteen pounds. Not knowing what to do, he walked into one last clinic. They told him he needed to get help. And like in all fairy tales and *telenovelas*, he woke up the next day in the hospital.

As Carlos and I were talking, Dr. Price came into the room with her ear-to-ear smile, Southern accent, and medical bag. She chatted with us as she propped his foot up to clean and debride it.

With sterile, surgical wrap on top, we are spared the details of a grisly reality beneath. As Dr. Price unwrapped the foot, Carlos's experience became real to me. To see what is missing is a shock. Beyond the heel, beyond a short portion where the foot was sliced off like a potato, there was nothing. The brief stump was dark and crusted. In the center was an oozing hole. As she rapidly plucked away bits of dead skin with tweezers, Dr. Price cheerfully asked Carlos if he had been able to put any weight on the foot. How did it feel to flex? Was it hurting?

He dutifully answered her questions, but his real concern was the unhealed hole in the center of the amputated surface. He was afraid that it wasn't healed because there was something inside. No, she assured him. It was healing well; it was only a surface problem, not infection, and would close.

Then he said, "But what I mean is, it feels like something is growing from the inside out, like part of my foot is moving to the outside, like it is growing a new little foot. It's weird," he frowned.

Dr. Price tried to explain how we grieve for a part of us that used to be there, a phantom limb.

As a nonmedical person, I never see injuries like this. When I looked at the flat surface of the stump, it disturbed me that part of his foot used to grow on his hip. The surgeon had grafted skin from Carlos's hip to cover the amputation. Not only his foot but also his hip and his psyche now had to heal.

I asked him if he had told his family. He said he had called Mexico and told his brother and sister, but asked them not to tell his mother about the foot. He said he would tell her in person when she could see that he was all right.

Later, as I got up to leave, Carlos said he would work on the job situation. He would spend time figuring out what kind of labor a forty-year-old man could do with one foot. He said, "I work. I don't beg."

Story Twenty

It was still dark when I arrived at the shed behind the church. Winter, 5:45 a.m. Your senses go into high gear when you are alone and in the dark. I looked around the parking lot to see if anyone was nearby, friend or foe. Even though the shed is behind the all-embracing Southside church, in the dark of the morning not everyone walking the alleys has generosity and equanimity in mind.

Usually more cars would be arriving, but today I was on my own. Two other volunteers had planned to go on patrol, but this morning at 5:30 one called to tell me he had the flu, and the other one had called the night before to say her child was sick. It's always a chore to arrange a schedule for these patrols, so I decided to go alone anyway.

I parked my truck so the headlights shined on the shed door, where you have to get down on your knees to fumble and cajole the key into the recessed lock of the big metal door. Whoever designed this system didn't consider the hard-earned dignity of human beings. I hadn't even started my trip and I was already dirty, knees in the damp soil, numb red cut fingers slamming against the edge of the cold metal lock. I loaded up the Rodeo with supplies—the darned things are heavy when you're alone—and headed out. Not able to resist that delicious sludgy Circle K coffee, I stopped to buy one for the road.

As I hit I-19 toward Nogales, I tuned into La Caliente, 102.1 FM on the radio, a Radio en Español channel, so I could keep in mind Spanish verbs and the general sense of *celebración* that come from an early morning radio show. All was well in this best of all possible worlds. I like traveling alone.

Almost to Arivaca Road; the sun was rising, cutting out a sharp silhouette of Elephant Head peak and Mount Wrightson. As I pulled into Amado, I saw a couple of Border Patrol trucks, the agents chatting by the side of the road. I turned and drove by some washes at the edge of town. Not seeing any fresh signs of people, I headed back and went to the town of Arivaca, passing the mercantile. For a moment, I thought of stopping and running in to get another coffee.

But I moved on, passing several sites in the Buenos Aires refuge, and randomly chose to go in at milepost 7. I parked by some trees, put on my backpack, and locked up the car. I headed down a trail west of the milepost marker, ducked under mesquite branches, scoured the path for fresh footprints. None. I made my way down a little hill into the first wash, looking around for signs. In the crisp morning air, I heard wind and crackles and chirps.

Years ago, the day after my divorce, I had walked here with Max, my Airedale. Not paying attention, we had almost bumped into a huge mesquite branch, jutting out into the wash so low I could have hit my head on it. With an astounding whoosh, out of proportion to the stillness, a mammoth owl lifted off the branch right in front of us, its dark wings bigger than solitude.

But at this moment there was no owl, no dog, no footprints. I resumed walking and began to call out in Spanish, "Hola, somos amigos . . ." Hello, we are friends, we have food, water. We come to help . . . Hello, we are friends, we have. . . . I walked and called for a long time. I was now in the Big Wash; thick trees bent to the sand, morning light filtered through leaves. I didn't see him at first. I don't know where he came from.

He was just there, ahead, walking rapidly toward me. I stopped. He moved fast. When he was a yard away, he demanded, "¿Estás sola?" Are you alone? I said, "Are you alone?" He said yes. I said my friends were back up the trail behind me. I kept my eyes on his eyes, but listened for any footsteps that might be joining us.

"What are you doing?" I asked.

"Walking," he said, smiling.

"Are you thirsty?" I broke into my Samaritan litany. "We have water and food. Are you hungry?"

"Yes."

I said, "Look, I'm with Samaritans, a group of volunteers. We're here to help give people water. How long have you been walking?"

"Four days."

I said come on, let's go sit under those trees.

We walked up a little trail and settled into a private spot behind thick bushes. He was like a piece of beef jerky—skinny and tough, five feet six inches tall, my height. His name was Armando. We sat. He didn't say anything. He watched carefully as I unzipped my pack. I pulled out the healthy but not terribly delicious items of food. He ate two whole packs of food and drank three bottles of water before he said anything. He had a bad eye that pointed the opposite direction from the good eye. I never know which one to look at. He had the tiniest mustache, maybe because he was eighteen, not twenty-two as he said.

"Aren't you traveling with other people?" I asked.

"Yes, but I don't know where they are."

"What happened?"

"We had a problem in the hills. There were gunshots. It was bad."

"What was bad?"

He drank more water, relaxing just a little but still tense, as if he were going to jump up and run. I told him a little about myself, thinking conversation would calm him down. He wasn't interested.

So I asked again, "What was bad?"

He had been with four other men. They were coming here to work. Starting in Mexico at sundown, they walked part of the night. After hours of walking, they came upon a bluff and hiked down the dark trail to the arroyo below to rest a little. There was no moonlight on this side of the overhang. As they were getting settled, they heard a vehicle drive up above them and could see lights reflected in the trees on the cliff. There must have been a road there at the top, he said. He heard voices of four men. Three were shouting and the fourth man was arguing back. Abruptly, Armando and his friends heard gunshots. Then there was silence. They heard a heavy thud and rocks and gravel started falling on their heads. Armando and his friends ran. He hid. When daylight came, he couldn't find his friends. He started walking.

"Were they speaking Spanish or English?"

"Spanish."

"Where did this happen?"

"P'alla," he said, waving his hand behind him. Way over there.

"Where exactly?"

"I don't know."

"Were you in Mexico or this side?"

"I don't know, it was dark," he said, exasperated.

"What were they yelling about?"

"I don't know. We could only hear a few words. They were angry."

"Well, who were they?"

He shrugged. "Bajadores."

I'd never heard the word.

"What?" I asked.

"Bajadores," he said, losing even more patience with me.

"I don't know that word. Describe it to me with other words."

"Bad men, sick men."

Oh. Lowlifes.

He drank even more water.

"Is there a town near here?" he asked.

"Arivaca, but some people there don't like migrants."

"How far?"

"About thirty-five minutes on foot."

He focused on me with his clear eye, then said, "For you thirty-five, for me fifteen."

I laughed. He said he just wanted to go home, near Hermosillo. He was married and wanted to see his five-month-old son. He said this had been a bad trip. He stood up. I gave him more water, which he slipped into his big black garbage bag. He picked up our trash and put it in my backpack. He slung his garbage bag over his back, said *mil gracias*, and walked away. I headed in the other direction.

Story Twenty-one

There is great variety to the women you might encounter in the desert. We come in many forms.

Three of us Samaritans were talking about egg rolls as we walked the trail. It was a hot June morning. We had hiked a couple of miles and were already talking about food.

Over to the left, something glistened. I glanced, but then it was gone. I remember thinking that I saw her out of the corner of my eye.

The prospect of warm homemade egg rolls in translucent wrappers made my mouth water. Arjahn Sarayut Arnanta, a Samaritan Buddhist monk from Thailand who likes to make a Thai egg roll, had brought enough egg rolls to feed the three of us. Norma, Arjahn, and I were on the Cerro Colorado trail about two miles from the nearest dirt road.

Arjahn explained that he once made egg rolls to take to Mariposa, the aid station just on the other side of the line where deported migrants are deposited by Border Patrol. He had made 300 for Mariposa. He and another Samaritan drove an hour and a half from Tucson to the border. Upon arrival, Arjahn looked in the box and found only 298 left. Although Arjahn never asked, the other Samaritan did mention she hadn't had breakfast before leaving Tucson.

He also told us he had taken the monastery dog to the veterinarian. After she finished giving the shots, the vet offered the dog a treat. He didn't want it. She said, "I've never seen a dog refuse these cookies. What do you feed him?"

"Thai food and egg rolls," answered Arjahn.

After another half mile, deep in conversation about delicious Thai goodies, we came to a rise and saw a line of seven people snaking single file up a trail. Behind them, as far as we could see, were mounds of cactus-covered hills, faint crisscrossing trails, and overhead a troublesome sun.

"¿Tiene suero?" was the first thing a man said as we approached. He was asking for rehydrating fluids, an IV. His name was Marcos. He was sweating and, as he staggered, another man reached out to help him. We were two miles from a road and had passed no shade. Our only choice for cooling them down was two scrawny mesquite trees up the steep hill behind us.

The group had been three days on the desert and stayed together when the pollero left with the rest of a large group, telling them to just stay on the trail. Not even the animals "just stay on the trail" because there is no single trail. Trails become tracks and then become nothing. Or suddenly they split, appendages twisting over a hill or down into a wash. One woman said that just before they saw us, they realized they had been walking in circles for days and were giving up hope.

Marcos's brother and another man helped Marcos up the hill to the trees and laid him down. Since our satellite phone was out of order, Norma walked up a hill to call the Arivaca Fire Department with her cell phone to give our GPS location for an ambulance. I stomped on the "cool packs" to kick them into "ice" mode and then placed them under Marcos's armpits. Arjahn removed his long outer saffron robe and threw it across the leafless branches to make shade. He said "I have been wearing this robe for over twenty years, and it is the first time in twenty years it has been useful—it is now for saving a life."

The group was composed of three men and two women who were sisters. One woman, Rosa, had two sons, eight and nine years old. They were all coming to prearranged jobs in the United States. As I got Marcos to take a few sips of water, I asked Pablo, the eight-year-old, where he was from. He just looked at me. I asked him if he had a girl-friend. He quickly put his face in his mother's lap and started laughing. Then both boys giggled and told Rosa that I talked funny. She smiled and said be polite, but my gringa accent was just too much for them. I kept talking, and soon everyone was laughing. I made a note to return to Spanish class.

Today as I write, I see Juan Diego, the Virgin of Guadalupe, and Saint Toribio Romo encircling my wrist. Nine more faces are lacquered onto tiny pieces of wood forming a bracelet I wear. While we were try-ing to make Marcos more comfortable, Rosa pulled Pablo to her and whispered in his ear. He came to me and held out his palm with two bracelets, one for me and one for Norma.

Although each person had been days on the desert and looked it—dirty clothes, dust on the hair and faces—Rosa was lovely. She was middle-aged, had a smile that just wouldn't leave. Her dark hair laced with gold highlights hung in layers; she had long red nails, was dressed in dark desert clothes, and wore sparkling earrings and bracelets. She sat very still, arms wrapped around her boys keeping them near.

Norma and Arjahn hiked out to get more supplies from our vehicle and to flag down the ambulance. I stayed with the group. Marcos was ill. His brother tended to him, but Marcos couldn't get off the ground without passing out. We propped up his head, tried to get him to drink some sips of water once in a while.

As I dabbed water on his face, I started to feel anxious. Behind me I felt a presence. When I glanced out beyond the shade, she was there. I saw her riding the heat, shimmering like a mirage on the edge of stillness. There was no form to her. There was no wind, nothing to reflect light, but I knew she was with us.

During childhood, I was carefully taught the stories of women who roam the desert looking for their loved ones and their children. La Llorona. Banshee. Ghost. Call them what you will. As I grew up, I realized they were stories to keep children from misbehaving—don't be bad or La Llorona will come. Don't look her in the eyes or she will take you away forever. I became an adult and quit believing in these women. But lately, as I spend more time on the desert, they have returned to my thoughts.

I spent a week camping on the desert with other volunteers. We were near sharp hills and rocky streambeds. One afternoon, a summer storm drenched us, thunder broke and washes roared. The sun went away, and as we prepared dinner in the dark, we heard a startling moan. It grew louder. Something was in great pain or distress. It sounded like an animal. Thinking that a cow had slipped and fallen into a crevasse during the storm, another woman and I took our flashlights and started walking toward the loud moaning. It was nerve-wracking. We walked a dirt road to the east. Then the sound seemed to come from the north. We took a trail north. But after ten minutes, the sound came from the south. We bushwhacked to the south but realized we could get lost in the darkness. We wanted to a least locate the cow, then contact some ranchers to take care of the animal. After winding around for an hour, chasing the disturbing cries, we saw light from our camp and returned. I got into my sleeping bag, listened to the moaning. I couldn't sleep until it stopped. In the morning, we looked around for a while but found nothing. Since childhood, I have known that in daylight, everything is different. That which is not real hides.

Arjahn returned to us with water. Norma waited for the ambulance two miles away at the road. The paramedics asked if they could drive up to where we were. There was no real road, just a wide flat area for some distance. Norma said she didn't think so because there were barbed-wire fences. She was concerned when the paramedic said, "Oh, we can just cut them," because she thought, what will happen to the cattle? The ambulance moved ahead and Norma jogged on to us.

I saw a helicopter flying in circles a few miles away. I went to the top of a hill and waved, trying to get their attention. I assumed it was the helicopter we had given GPS coordinates, but they were so far to the south that I thought perhaps it was just an ICE copter looking for migrants. Finally, it circled directly overhead; I waved my arms. I shouted to the people under the tree that they were here. The copter circled a few times, lowered close to us, then left.

From the hill, I could see the ambulance inching toward us. Then Norma returned. We saw the helicopter again. We waved from the hill-top. The normally dignified Norma took off her white blouse, waved it in broad strokes, jumping up and down. Eventually it saw us, came near, and we realized it was a different helicopter. It, too, left.

Then I looked across the hills. When the ambulance was a football field away, to my complete astonishment smoke suddenly exploded up from the front of the vehicle, like a special-effects trick in an action movie.

A young volunteer EMT in full firefighting gear jogged to us from the stranded ambulance. Unfortunately he didn't have IV equipment we needed, so we prepared to carry Marcos down the trail to the road where our Samaritan vehicle was.

From the stranded vehicle, the Arivaca Fire Department solicited the help of the Green Valley Paramedics, forty-five minutes away. So as we prepared to leave, two paramedics arrived from our trail to the west. Simultaneously, a Border Patrol BORSTAR agent and a man in civilian clothes arrived on a trail from the east.

Marcos sat up, talked a little, but couldn't stand. The BORSTAR agent tried to start an IV. He couldn't find the vein, kept jabbing both of Marcos's arms until Marcos said no, don't do it again. The agent explained that his abilities were hampered because he had just returned from his honeymoon the night before and wasn't really ready to be back at work. One of the paramedics took over and started the IV.

Then the man who accompanied the agent got down on his knees in front of us. He pulled a camera out of his bag and began shooting photos of me next to Marcos, who had his head down and an IV in his arm. I said you can't take photos without permission. His face hardened, and he stared at us for a long moment. His words measured by anger, he said, "Whose permission?" I said Marcos's, and I inquired who he was. He said he was a doctor. I said, From where, and why are you taking photos? He said he was a Tucson emergency room doctor and was taking photos to use for teaching purposes. He reluctantly put the camera away. He said, "I didn't ask permission because I can't speak Spanish." I said, "I could have translated for you."

The Border Patrol agent said he had called for a helicopter to carry Marcos to the hospital, had called for more agents to take the family into custody, and would meet us at our vehicle on the road. Eventually the Green Valley paramedics put Marcos's arms over their shoulders and carried him out, accompanied by the photographer and the agent. We explained that the trail they were going to take was the longest route. He insisted they would arrive before we did.

We all gathered the family's belongings and started down the trail, passed the disabled Arivaca emergency vehicle, and walked toward the road. Rosa patted her son on the head, and her sister guided the other boy. Exhaustion not withstanding, Rosa was constantly vigilant with her boys, not letting them out of her sight. She was aware of the danger that shadowed them.

After we had walked a burning mile and a half, we heard someone shout at us, "Hold up, wait, they're under arrest!" We turned to look and saw the BORSTAR agent huffing and puffing toward us. He yelled, "You can't take them!" We said, "We know. We are just walking to the road." He said, "They are all in custody." We said, "Look at them—they aren't going anywhere. They can barely walk." He relaxed after he saw that they moved slowly and with effort. He cheered up and said, "My wife will be happy that I had this run. She wants me in better shape." He chatted away as we all struggled the last mile in the one hundred-degree heat.

Just before we arrived at the road, we came upon a yellow helicopter, the pilot, and a nurse. They were waiting to carry Marcos to the hospital in Tucson. They said they couldn't land earlier because if the brush is more than a foot high, it is sucked up into the blades, disabling the helicopter.

When we arrived at the road, the family sat on the ground, exhausted. We pulled out more food and cold water for everyone. A half hour later, Border Patrol vehicles came to take the family to a deportation center near Nogales. More than an hour after that, the Border Patrol vehicle arrived with Marcos and the paramedics. The doctor/photographer was driving. We asked why it had taken so long. "We got lost," the doctor said angrily, and drove over to the helicopter. We watched as Marcos was loaded onto the helicopter. It lifted off, a huge cloud of dust, rocks, and debris flying everywhere.

And that was when she returned to my thoughts. Through the dust I could see her. I could tell that she was dreaming. We all understand. I have had the dream; so have you. She is asleep and dreams. She dreams that something is wrong, something is missing. She starts to wake but can't climb to consciousness. She can't remember what is missing. She looks around. She looks in her bag. It is not there. She walks into the bedroom, but it is not there either. She looks under the bedcovers. No, not there. She walks outside and goes to the mesquite tree. She walks around the big trunk. It's not there. She steps onto the sandy trail, but can't find it. Then, ahead on the trail, she sees it. The shoe. She runs to pick it up, the dried gray canvas shoe. It is her son's shoe. She wakes. There is no shoe. There is no son. He is dead. He died there, just off the trail. She has to find him. She searches for eternity, looking for her son at night, hiding from the living during the day. If we are lucky, we won't see her but will leave our tears behind to let her know that we know.

Story Twenty-two

Over there, navy-blue mountains are barely visible. Closer to us, the low hills are weighted down with charcoal clouds. Closer yet is the silhouette of a naked mesquite tree, black arms supporting eleven vultures on this cold winter dawn. A light rain falls. As we search in the Buenos Aires refuge, we walk nearer to the birds. This morning we are in the sorcerer's home, moving through the mist.

Hunched-back vultures, sitting in a row, wing touching wing, pull their feathered coats up around the neck, their normally crimson heads now hidden in shadow. Everything operates by intuition this gray morning, with no direct light to point the way.

The vultures are silent, watching, their vision ten times more acute than ours. Though their wings carry them far, their feathers are light as air. In ancient Egypt, when someone died, the heart of the deceased was weighed against a vulture feather. If the heart was heavy with wickedness, it outweighed the feather and the soul of the deceased was eaten by the jackal, Anubis. If the heart was as light as the feather, the soul moved to the next life.

The vultures sit. We watch for the coyote, our southwestern Anubis, transporter of hearts and souls. We are surrounded by deep silence, a highly sought commodity by friend and foe. Looking into dark lairs covered with branches, we search.

Ted

Photograph by Steve Johnston

Previous page: Man climbs into "dog catcher" vehicle after apprehension by Border Patrol. (Courtesy of No More Deaths)

Story Twenty-three

I awoke this morning early and left for the shed a little after 6:00 a.m. The dawn is coming earlier now as the earth begins to tilt toward the sun in the northern climes, and everything is ghostly bluish as I pedal the few short blocks to the church. At the shed one of my companions from last week is loading the truck. The third of our party arrives, and we are together again the same as last week, three musketeers, or stooges, depending on your point of view.

One of our party saw on the news that it was raining west of the Baboquivaris last night and suggests we head out to the Tohono O'odham Nation to look for those in need of dry clothes and warm blankets.

We drive out Route 86. West of Three Points the road is wet with last night's rain. We see hardly a soul on the highway and no migrants in need, and after an hour of driving we head back to the junction of 286 and go south toward Mexico. We drive into Brown Canyon, park, and hike in a ways. We see recent signs of migrants passing this way, the footprints of their tennis shoes leaving sign cut into the trail.

Farther south and at the crossroads of Arivaca Road and Route 286 the Border Patrol is loading up a big bus. We stop to offer food and water, and the Border Patrol agent says fine. I count twenty-one souls lined up single file waiting to load; there are three women with the group. We carry the food packs over, and each migrant takes a pack from me as they step into the bus. It is a very young group. I guess their ages to be in the late teens, and certainly none appears to be over thirty years. They are laughing and in very good spirits, and we find out they had been out in the desert only one night before being caught. It almost seems as if they are on a high school field trip without the teacher chaperone.

My companion offers food and water to the Border Patrol agents, and one accepts, which she says is a first. She asks if there are any other detainees, and the agent points to three trucks parked nearby. We walk over, and this group is older than the group they are loading on the bus. They had been walking two days, and the atmosphere is much different. Two of the men are sitting on the ground and are crying. An SUV is stuffed with seven migrants, and three who are sitting together on the passenger bench seat watch as we approach. We offer food and water, and the three shake their heads no. Their eyes betray a deep-seated frustration and anger. I tell them the food and water are free, and they still refuse to take it.

It seems they want nothing from the gringo except the opportunity to clean his toilets, repair his roofs, and harvest the bountiful crops that the gringo is too lazy to do himself. Their eyes seem to say, "Why are we chased like animals and treated like criminals? You come offering your pitiful little plastic bag of crackers, Vienna sausages, and Jell-O pudding. Why don't you really help us and allow us to live and work in your rich country that throws away as garbage in a day what could feed my country for a week?" I have no answers for these questioning looks.

The Border Patrol has four-wheel-drive pickup trucks that appear to be dogcatcher vehicles. They transport migrants they have captured in the back of these metal shells. You can only stoop inside of them, and the seats are metal. An agent opens the back of his cage; eight migrants are crammed inside. They accept the offer of food and water.

We continue on our journey and go check out an abandoned trailer in which thirty-eight migrants including a baby were discovered hiding a few weeks ago by a group of Samaritans picking up trash. Trash pickup is a community service Samaritans offer to private landowners and on public lands.

In this case a person went over to check out what appeared to be an abandoned trailer with a bunch of trash around it, and when she started to open the door someone inside shut it. They peered in the window, and a pair of eyes peered back. The coyote was very nervous but allowed food and water to be distributed.

When we arrive, we walk over and shout out, but there is no answer. The trailer is empty of people. It is filled, however, with the stench of human waste. It is beyond filthy. I wonder how often it is has been used on this smuggling route and who owns it.

Of course it has no plumbing or electrical systems, and the migrants are hiding in there all day long. They can't go outside or risk being spotted. In the summer it would be unbearable, and yet they do bear it. We continue on our journey and see nothing more but the silent desert.

Story Twenty-four

Rain and snow came to the desert in the form of a fast-moving storm that originated way up in the northern climes. It is brutal in its cold swiftness. On Sunday morning the newspapers report that four migrants are dead from hypothermia or exposure, and scores have been sent to the hospital.

The mountains surrounding Tucson are beautiful when the snow level drops, and that morning all the major ranges had a dusting of snow down to six thousand feet. They sparkle in the morning sunlight, and from the warm environs of the house they beckon my granddaughter to ask her Tito if he will take her to the snow so she can play.

For a person walking through the night in the desert with clothes that are wet and temperatures dropping to the upper thirties along with winds in the twenty to thirty miles per hour range, the weather is deadly. Fatigue, exhaustion, dehydration, and hunger, the bane of migrants who have been traveling in the desert, will cause them to succumb more readily when exposed to the cold. The core temperature of the body drops. The muscles spasm uncontrollably, creating friction and therefore heat. As the inside of the body cools, this shivering may stop, and the arms and legs no longer have blood moving through them. The body begins to shut down, conserving precious heat. A person will exhibit poor speech, nausea, dizziness, poor judgment, apathy, and then finally stupor to unconsciousness in severe hypothermia. The blood pressure and respiratory rate fall, and the heart will try and pump the cold blood to someplace warm. The heartbeat flutters and then stops.

Treatment is basic and straightforward: remove the wet clothing and warm the body. Do not massage the extremities, since this may cause the heart to start beating wildly as small pools of warm blood where you have rubbed begin to push cold blood into and through the heart.

On Friday and Saturday in southern Arizona, those unfortunate souls who had no Weather Channel, no radio or daily news, just the clothes on their backs, some water in a gallon jug, and a few personal belongings in a backpack were walking north as the storm clouds gathered, temperatures dropped, and the cold hard rain came without warning. By the time my little granddaughter asked me to take her to the snow, those who would die were dead. There were four known. There were the unknown, never to be discovered, who lost their lives looking for a job.

A good friend constantly reminds me that all work has dignity, whether it's digging a ditch or teaching algebra. I wonder if a country that forces its laborers to cross its border on life-threatening journeys for a job has any dignity left.

Our borders have continually been used as a gate to keep out those of a lower status. Allow enough of them in to keep the labor pool cheap and expendable but not too many as to put a drain on social services or anger those who are afraid of people of color.

I received a call from a fellow Samaritan late Sunday afternoon asking if I would be willing to travel early Monday morning. I agreed. I awoke before dawn to find all the cars in my neighborhood covered with a thick frost. I met him at the church. Two women from out of town were to accompany us. They seemed pleasant enough. We drove out to the desert the usual way and saw nothing but Border Patrol zooming by at high speed on the two-lane blacktop road. The rain was welcome in this desert. The fine dust was packed tight with moisture so that old footprints were obliterated and the ground was too hard to take new ones, at least that the untrained eye could see.

We walked a trail in Brown Canyon and saw many signs of people having camped under mesquite trees whose branches were bent low. I worried what we might find in these camps, but thankfully no bodies lay dead upon the desert floor.

Later on the blacktop we saw a big Homeland Security bus on the side of the road. A young woman standing solo, waiting to be boarded, looked lost and forlorn. The agents would not let us give her food and water, and we could not tell if there were others inside. Farther south, more men squatted by the road, waiting for the big bus.

We traveled through Arivaca and came upon three men on the side of the road resting in the now warm sun. They were tired and hungry, having been walking since Sunday morning after the rain and snow had stopped. They had crossed the border on their own without a coyote to guide them.

We talked about the options for them, let them know how far they still had to walk, and told them where they were in relation to Tucson and Phoenix.

They discussed their situation and then asked me to call Border Patrol. Their English was very good. As we waited for the Border Patrol I asked them their story. Neto told me they were all from the state of Guanajuato in Mexico. He had a wife and five children living in Los Angeles and had returned to Mexico because his father was very ill; he wanted to see him before he died. He now wanted to be reunited with his wife and kids. Jorge had returned to his village after working in the Denver area for three years so he could see his children and wife. There was no work in Guanajuato; so he was on his way back to Denver. Francisco had returned because he had not seen his wife and kids in ten years. He has been living and working in the Denver area like Jorge and now needed to find work, for there was none in Mexico.

The Border Patrol came to pick them up in a little van. The officer was as brown as these usual suspects. I wondered how the officer and his family came to be here. I wondered about the American Indian who was outnumbered and eventually conquered and subjected to rule by a horde of European illegal aliens. And I wondered if one day the white man would be overrun and subjected to rule by these hard-working people from the south and if this was why in the current paradigm white people were so paranoid.

We shook their hands and wished them good luck, then headed back to Tucson, the sun warming the desert.

In Green Valley, a retirement community south of Tucson, a large group of migrants were in custody on the frontage road by the side of the freeway. They were too many to count. It was next to a golf course with houses all over the place. I imagine some terrified citizen saw them hiding and called the Border Patrol, not realizing these people were the ones who cooked in the club house, mowed the fairways, trimmed the weeds, and would repair the roofs of the houses that lined the golf course in the years to come.

Story Twenty-five

Today I travel with two experienced Samaritans. One of my companions has a very good sixth sense and guides us to an area I've never been before as a Samaritan. We look for migrant sign and come across some fresh water bottles and footprints. We notice a truck coming up fast. We get back in our truck and start cruising, and a Border Patrol agent passes us, does a U-turn, goes back to where we were, and checks out the migrant signs we were looking at. This area must see a lot of traffic, since it's on the east side of the Altar Valley and the migrants can pass this way on trails hugging the low mountains on their way into Tucson proper.

The road eventually plays out, and as we head back toward Route 286 we spot a helicopter cruising up the road we saw the Border Patrol agent on.

We continue south toward the border and turn west onto a ranch road. A Border Patrol agent is coming out, and we stop him. We ask him what the Border Patrol uses on the GPS as way points. He tells us, then adds a warning to be careful—all the action is down near Arivaca today.

We pass through a gate and find a trail with fresh tracks. We load up with food and water and walk north. We see no one, and the day is perfect for a stroll through the desert. My companions discuss the charges filed against two young people who were arrested nine months ago for transporting three migrants. Their arrest was what brought me to Samaritans.

The wheels of justice turn slowly for these two. The date for their trial has been set and vacated twice in the last four months. It may be quite a while before the case goes to trial, if it ever does. (On September 1, 2006, indictments against Daniel Strauss and Shanti Sellz were dismissed by federal judge Raner Collins. The judge cited evidence of "selective prosecution" as reason for his dismissal, and said the two had been following guidelines that border volunteers had been using for several years without being arrested.)

As for the three migrants, justice, or the lack thereof, was swift. One was detained for six weeks so the federal prosecutor and defense attorney could get a statement and then was deported, while the other two were deported immediately. The testimony of those two will never be a factor, as no one really knows who they are or where they went.

We head south on 286, and I pick up the local paper (*Arizona Daily Star*, March 15, 2006) that is lying at my feet and see three articles about the nearby border: "Entrant held; his child died in chase," "Marijuana smuggler killed by gunfire was Mexican, 23," and "Sanctuary policies may cancel aid to cities."

The first article is about a migrant who was crossing with his twelve-year-old daughter. They were with some others on the third day of the journey when a Border Patrol agent spotted the group and started chasing them in his truck. Everyone ran. According to a report by the Yuma County Attorney's Office, the agent gave chase and after the migrants stopped, the agent got out of his truck, heard moaning, and discovered he had run over this man and his daughter. She died. The migrant was charged with child endangerment, since it was argued that he had placed the child at risk of imminent death by bringing her into the desert. He had been sitting in jail for the past week. "They said it's my fault for bringing her here, that it's my fault my daughter died," he said. "But I wasn't driving the truck; I just wanted her to get a good education." He had been heading for Oxnard, California, where his wife was living with their two-month-old son. He had wanted to enroll his daughter in school and continue his work in the area's strawberry fields. The sheriff's detectives determined that the death was an accident, so the Border Patrol agent would face no punishment.

The second article is typical in that most of the facts are left out. The driver of an SUV picked up a wounded Mexican, took him to the hospital, then left. The wounded man was in a group of men carrying packs of marijuana. Someone yelled out "stop" in English and then opened fire. The sheriff's department does not even know where the shooting occurred, just somewhere near the road between Amado and Arivaca, and "asks that the driver of the SUV come forward for questioning." Fat chance of that.

The third article is a perfect example of just how divisive the whole issue of migration has become. A bill in the Arizona House of

Representatives passed and is on the way to the Senate that would deny state revenues to cities and counties that have "any sanctuary policy." This ranges from programs that provide aid to people or any restricted enforcement by local police of federal laws that make it a crime to be in this country illegally.

The sponsor of the bill is quoted as saying, "Sanctuary policies kill Americans, kill police officers every day by allowing violent criminal aliens to remain in communities. The largest and most violent gangs in America are made up of illegals."

In our present political environment, it would not be a stretch to conceive of enforcement using the color of someone's skin as probable cause for questioning of a person's citizenship.

We continue south and then east on Arivaca Road. We stop again at my companions' urging at a spot I had checked out only once quite a while ago. It is a heavily wooded area with big desert willows, cottonwoods, and mesquite alongside a deep arroyo. We begin to walk and shout out our Samaritan greetings. The trail has recent signs of foot traffic. I notice a faint trail branching off and leading up a short incline and follow this. At the top of the incline it levels out and the trees are thick. The trail plays out, and one of my companions says, "Hey, check this out."

Under a tree is a gunnysack. I bend over to pick it up. One of my companions says, "Wait a second. Are we alone?" I can't see anything but the gunnysack, and my companions look around as I investigate. It is extremely light. But it does have something in it. I open it and dump out five more gunnysacks and the short lengths of twine used to close the top. I open the other bags and find nothing is in them. They are all empty. I smell them. Just moldy gunnysack smell. We laugh short little nervous laughs and make light of the find. The sacks are used by what are called mules, but are people, to carry drugs from Mexico into the United States.

We continue on about a mile and a half up the main trail to the crest of a hill that is littered with hundreds of plastic bottles and not much else. I imagined migrants and smugglers tossing the extra water bottles aside, since the highway was now in sight and the journey nearly over.

On our return to the truck, one companion thought we should put the gunnysacks back the way we found them. We did so as to not disturb what some might construe as a crime scene and also to keep our profile as low as possible. No need for whoever put the sacks there to know someone discovered them.

We continued on our patrol and for the day saw not one migrant in custody nor any wandering about the countryside.

Norma

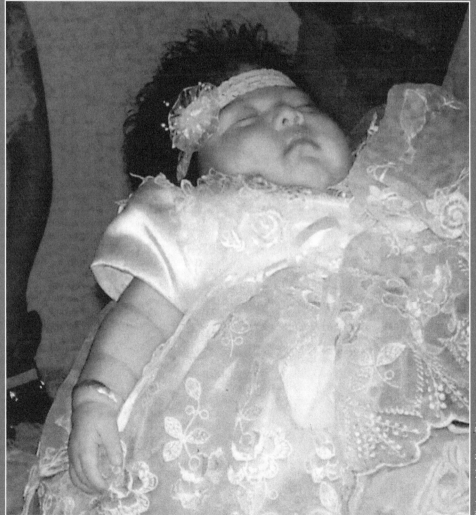

Photograph by Norma Price

Previous page: Veronica's baptism.

Story Twenty-six

Miracle Baby, that's Veronica. It was early summer, and I had just spent the afternoon holding that little creature, born on the desert floor of southern Arizona, among saguaro, cholla, prickly pear cacti, and creosote bushes. She was not yet three weeks old and already had an aura of strength and independence. Plump little cheeks, eyes closed, and body bouncing rhythmically with rapid breathing. Her head, chockfull of jet-black hair, glossy and beautiful. I reached down to touch her fingers, and she stirred with a whimper, then began to fidget and yawn. She stretched and drifted back into the land of angels and fairies.

That is when I learned firsthand about the baby born in the desert, with survivor engraved on her soul. Veronica's mother, twenty-five-year-old Ana, was from Guatemala but had been living and working in Chiapas when she decided she had to leave and come north. Chiapas is Mexico's southernmost state and shares a border with Guatemala. Ana thought she was only seven months pregnant. Her group had been crossing the desert several days, had slept on the ground three nights. Ana went into the bushes to go to the bathroom. Others in her group called out for her to be careful, to be on the lookout for snakes and bandits. There were no snakes or bandits, but she felt a pain in the front of her abdomen, down low, and squatted to defecate. During labor of her two previous pregnancies she had had pain in her lower back, but never in the front part of her abdomen. This pain was different. Then, two more pains in the lower, anterior abdomen, and she felt the baby coming. Immediately her baby cried out. On hearing that high-pitched wail, two other women in the group ran to her, took the baby, cleaned it, and wrapped it in a soft T-shirt. They cut the umbilical cord with fingernail clippers.

The rest of the group left the three women and moved on northward. The two impromptu midwives then took a shawl and bound the infant to the mid-body of the mother and the four of them began a trek toward the highway, three miles away. A Border Patrol helicopter spotted the small group—three "undocumented" crossers and one U.S.–born baby. A call to the ground alerted Border Patrol agents. They arrived on the scene, efficiently evacuated the mother by helicopter, and transported the infant by ambulance to the hospital. The two *comadres* were immediately arrested and returned to Mexico by the Border Patrol.

We asked Ana about all the attention she had received. We had heard that she had refused press interviews and photos. We thought her very wise to avoid all of the media exposure. "What did the reporters say?" we asked her.

"I wouldn't talk with them because my eyes and face were puffy and I hadn't washed my hair yet," she told us shyly in Spanish.

All three Samaritans were grandmothers, and each of us wanted to hold this special baby. Are these creatures, who are brought into this life in environments less favorable to survival, stronger in order to endure? This tiny survivor slept soundly. She only stirred and woke to nurse or have a diaper change, and then went back to dreamland: no colic, no crying to be held, no fretting at 3:00 a.m.

However, the beautiful newborn had a problem. She did not possess a birth certificate. The two women who cleaned the infant and helped Ana and Veronica to the road were gone, so they could not verify the time and location of the birth. So began the cycle of bureaucratic red tape.

Ana had left her backpack in the care of the comadres who assisted the delivery. They were immediately deported, and phone calls to Nogales said the women had moved on and were no longer at the shelter in that border town. All of Ana's belongings, including identification papers and phone numbers, had been in her *mochila*.

Back in Guatemala, Ana's mother did not know that she was a new *abuela* and had a brand-new *nieta*. She did not even know whether Ana was dead or alive. Ana, knowing neither how to read nor write, had never used a phone card. But that would not have helped anyway, since there was no telephone in the home where Ana's mother lived.

Veronica's baptism was scheduled for the following Sunday at 4:00 p.m. Everyone was abuzz with anticipation. Rosalie, the godmother-to-be, had bought a christening dress for the baby and matching shoes for those tiny feet. She herself was as excited as a seven-year-old child the week before Christmas. A Mexican American and devout Catholic, she remembered the christening of each one of her own six children. The bishop was going to baptize Veronica in the cathedral. I am not Catholic, and emotionally I did not feel the impact of this, but intellectually I felt its significance. I was moved that the bishop would accommodate his schedule to baptize the daughter of an unmarried peasant woman from two thousand miles away. He is a humble man, and even with all the demands and important functions of his office he always has shown compassion for fellow human beings, regardless of their station in life.

Rosalie told me that Ana had been chatting with her and was opening up more about her feelings. She had talked about her experience in the hospital. Someone in white came into her room. She didn't know if it was a doctor or nurse. The person in white began talking to her in a sensitive, sympathetic way. She told Ana that adoption of her baby would be possible if she wanted to consider it. Ana remained expressionless and did not respond. The medical person affectionately touched her arm. "Just think about it. I'll be back tomorrow," she said. Ana did think about it. When Veronica's father had found out that Ana was pregnant, he vanished. Then Ana had doubts about the pregnancy. Should she have this baby or not? She took herbal abortifacients without any result. There was no miscarriage from the home remedies; she didn't even get sick. Still pregnant, she headed north. She could earn more money in the United States than she had earned working in a restaurant in Chiapas. There were friends and a possible job in Florida, where she planned to pick fruit. She needed to send money home to her mother for the care of her other two children, now orphaned by the shove of economic deterioration in Guatemala and the sucking force of available employment in the United States. There in the hospital she thought about another mouth to feed, one more responsibility, one more anxiety. She considered the offer from the kindly, sterile person in white. The next day she had her answer ready: "No, I want to keep my baby."

Rosalie had noticed a change in the attitude and mannerisms of mother toward baby in the previous weeks. Ana had always been very attentive to the needs of the infant, feeding, changing, and caring for her. But during the past ten days Rosalie noticed how Ana tickled the baby under the chin and said "goo-goo" baby words, cooing and gushing over Veronica. It was a change. This type of attentiveness had not previously been in the repertoire between mother and child. Rosalie was aware of the lack of affectionate silliness so prevalent in the way Americans act toward babies. Maybe the behavior pattern in *campesino* mothers is more stoic. They rise early, up before daybreak, to get to the fields to pick fruit or vegetables. The older women—grandmothers, great-aunts, and other village crones—are the ones who stay home to raise and care for babies and young children. They are the ones who interact daily with the youngsters while the mothers are off in the fields. Rosalie wondered if Ana's seeming maternal aloofness was a cultural influence, maybe lack of a role model. Or was it, in fact, that Ana wasn't sure about wanting to keep little Veronica, who would complicate her life even more? Now, unable to work, she had spent more time with her daughter, a situation not previously possible with her other two children. After weeks of constant interaction, she had bonded with her child.

On the morning of the christening we stood at the rear of St. Augustine's Cathedral, quietly chatting. Only one of the five of us had ever been here before, and we were discussing the spiritual simplicity of the space. Most other Catholic churches I had visited were very ornate in design and décor, but St. Augustine's Cathedral is not ornate; it is a church of the people. I looked up. Weavings high on the walls were of a contemporary motif: brown and white hands reaching toward each other, and another of children singing. Almost to the ceiling, the sun shone purple through the central panel of stained-glass windows. The light streaming through filled the sanctuary with warmth.

The doors on each side of the sanctuary were flanked by wood-carved statues of saints. No marble statues. No gold leaf or frescoes. At the front of the church was a large statue of a risen Christ. No agonal Jesus on a cross with blood streaming down his face from pricks of a thorny crown. It was a welcoming Jesus Christ with hands outstretched toward you, calling all to come to him.

The door behind us opened and Rosalie entered, carrying a bundle of white organdy and lace. In the crook of her arm was a round face topped with a huge tuft of jet-black hair. On top of the silky black bristles was a tiara of white bows and lace. Two chubby little cheeks peeked out, brushed with black eyelashes. Rosalie beamed. No abuela was ever more proud of her charge. Ana followed with a serene half-smile, a childlike mother herself. She had just talked with her mother on the telephone, the first conversation they had had in many months, and she had told her of the new nieta, born in the desert.

As other friends arrived and moved into our circle, little Veronica was passed from one to the other. Oohs and ahhs were interrupted by a somber man who beckoned us, twelve in all, to come forward to the baptismal font where the bishop waited.

As we assembled in the transept, the bishop asked a few questions and said a few introductory words in English. Then the sacrament began in Spanish. Again I was moved by this man of God, this bishop of Lebanese heritage, speaking to a humble Guatemalan woman in her native tongue.

Veronica was quiet and well-behaved during the entire ceremony, but then I had never heard her cry much anyway. The bishop said the ceremonial words and poured water over the baby's head as Rosalie tilted Veronica down toward the basin. A non-Catholic woman asked Sister Audrey, one of two nuns in attendance, "Is it unusual for the bishop to be performing a baptism?" Sister Audrey said definitely so. The bishop, she added, has many other responsibilities, and the parish priest usually carries out the functions of the church.

The ceremony ended. The group moved toward the front of the church for photographs. Meanwhile, others, tourists or seekers of peace and solace, had come into the cathedral and were praying silently or wandering around. As the bishop completed the sacrament, visitors came forward to see Veronica and exclaim over her. Veronica Milagro, she had been christened. Veronica the little miracle.

Story Twenty-seven

Beatriz crossed the border at Sasabe. She traveled alone in the desert for twenty-three days. Injured and with no provisions, she made her way north, drinking water she found in discarded water jugs and eating cactus fruit. Day after day she struggled along looking for others. "I could not believe there were no other people." Her face was emotionless as she told her story.

That her odyssey occurred during early May was her salvation. The killing heat had not yet arrived in southern Arizona.

Early in her journey, soon after crossing the border, Beatriz fell. She stepped over a rock, twisted her foot, and fractured bones in her ankle. She tried to hobble along with her group, but it was soon evident that she could not keep up and was slowing them down. They moved on, leaving her with a small amount of food and a bottle of water. "I found a tree limb to use as a *bastón*," she said, and leaning on it for support, she continued onward. She passed old campsites where migrants had tossed aside clothes and personal items. At night she lay down in the arroyos and covered herself with the discarded clothing. By day she slowly moved from one campsite to another.

These sites are where migrants sleep when the polleros let them rest. The trees provide cover, and there is a lot of green in summertime, a scarcity in the desert. The vegetation provides cooling shade and conceals them from Border Patrol helicopters that fly low over the terrain, skimming the top of the trees. But these beautiful, shady spots are littered with trash. Samaritans hold regular "cleanup" days, on both public and private lands, to help clear the littered, cluttered sites.

Every discarded item has a story behind it. Scattered in shrubbery near the half-empty jugs of water, toiletries, and backpacks, there are lacy bras in red and lavender, toothbrushes, deodorant, razors, cologne, and lipstick. There are airline and bus ticket receipts, birth certificates, wedding and family photos. Then there are the diapers, baby clothes, and toddler shoes. I have found Bibles, the Book of Mormon, porno comic books, and toys at these sites. When their ride comes, the migrants leave everything behind. The coyotes pack as many people into a vehicle as possible, but passengers must discard their belongings. The polleros do not want any added weight. Low-riding vehicles would betray them to the Border Patrol. Besides, the passengers are headed for a new life. They anticipate new jobs. No need to cling to the clothes from previous times.

The camps that Beatriz passed and where she spent the nights were far from any road, and there were not as many discarded items, just a few pieces of clothing that she took to cover herself against the night chill. Beatriz would scavenge campsites for water left in jugs, no matter how meager the amount. On one occasion she found a *charco*, a small puddle. To her it did not look filthy, but she got sick after drinking from the stagnant pool. She stayed in that area for about five days hoping someone else would appear. No one did. Foraging for something to eat, she collected the thick, tender young pads of the prickly pear cactus. She would strip off the thorns and eat the juicy green plants, her main source of food. These cactus pads, called nopales, were a staple of the Native American diet for many years.

At one point Beatriz came upon a house surrounded by old, rusted cars. She could barely walk and was making no progress. "I called out, then went in the house, and no one was there. I got something to eat from the kitchen, and decided to wait until someone came. Maybe they would help me."

Then she looked at her surroundings. There were photos of men with guns, lots of them. Who lived here? Were they vigilantes or maybe hunters? Unsure of the significance of the photos, she was afraid to remain in the house. It might be a meeting place for some group that hated migrants. She decided not to stay; she would move on and take her chances.

Her limping, stumbling journey continued. One night she met two young men on the trail who were headed north. They helped her climb to the top of a ridge where they pointed out lights in the distance; this gave her hope. The men had a long way to go and told her she weighed too much for them to carry. They said they were afraid to linger and risk being apprehended themselves, but they gave her some of their food and water, called out "Dios la bendiga," God bless you, and disappeared into the darkness. She inched on toward the lights, every step more painful than the previous one. Finally she resorted to moving on her knees, even as pilgrims at churches all over Mexico crawl on their knees toward the image of the Virgin of Guadalupe, seeking blessings or doing penance. They too are left with bruised and bloodied kneecaps.

Beatriz took a scrap of carpet from a trash pile, and put it on the ground to pad her knees. Again she moved forward, and the crusty scabs were scraped off as she put first one knee and then the other on the carpet. One knee was bleeding and the other was covered by a patchy, purple scab with yellowish fluid oozing from under the crust. Beatriz made the rest of her "pilgrimage" that way, knees on the carpet, inching forward. By the time she had reached the road, both knees were a blackish-purple pulp. Tiny rocks and grit had become embedded into the tissues. Vertical lacerations dissected the skin over her patellas. In the middle of each leg where her knees should have been were large overripe purple figs, bulging with pulp and oozing juice from linear splits in the skin.

"When I reached the road I waited, hoping someone would stop to help," she said. Car after car passed by without stopping. At last, a Mexican American man, probably a rancher, stopped to see if she needed help.

"Mija, es mojada?" "Dear, are you a wetback?" he asked. She said yes, and that she couldn't walk. "Don't worry my child; I will call an ambulance." He told her to wait fifteen minutes and he would return. True to his word, he came back, and an ambulance arrived soon after. She was taken to the hospital where she was treated for severe dehydration, her knees were cleaned, X-rays were taken, and she underwent surgery on her fractured ankle.

Beatriz had left Chiapas after Hurricane Stan devastated the land and crops and many jobs were lost. Chiapas is one of the poorest states in Mexico. Half of the 3.5 million people are without potable or running water. For 90 percent of the families in the state, the family income is less than half of the minimum wage. Beatriz had no children but helped support her family, including her mother, siblings, nieces, and nephews. Her father was elderly and ill, and they needed her earnings to supplement the family income. When the hurricane hit the Pacific coast of Guatemala and Chiapas in 2005, all of the fields were flooded, no produce could be harvested, and all agricultural jobs were lost. Everyone headed north to work.

Beatriz said that the thing that kept her going, that gave her strength and energy to continue, was the memory of her mother when she left home. Close to her heart, she kept the image of her mother standing at the doorway, wet-eyed, rosary in her swollen, gnarled hands.

Story Twenty-eight

Child's drawing found on trail in desert.

L ittle Jessica stood with her mother and eight other migrants on a bare area of roadside. Her mother appeared much more frightened than four-year-old Jessica. The others squatting on the ground just looked tired and discouraged. The Border Patrol agent in charge gave us permission to hand a toy to the child. Her eyebrows lifted just millimeters and the hint of a smile curved the corners of her mouth. We handed granola bars and peanuts to the others while Holly, our Spanish speaker, talked with the young mother. She was very anxious. She and Jessica had been separated from her husband when the group was apprehended, and she did not know if she would even see him again, so she told Holly.

While we stood there with the tired group, a huge Blackhawk helicopter landed in the middle of the road. A group disgorged from the giant bird, and Jessica's father headed in our direction, plastic bands locking his wrists, like handcuffs. Tears ran down the mother's face. It was a reunion of relief rather than one of joy.

The three of us, all women, wondered at the stamina not just of the children, but of the parents who bring them. It is no easy task taking care of babies and children in the most foreseeable conditions. How do they manage the unpredictable journey through the harsh desert? The previous week there had been children on the Homeland Security bus, but I was never allowed to see them. That day we pulled over and asked the bus driver if we could give the migrants food and water. "No," he said, and then added: "We don't have many here. Just a woman with two kids and two other men."

The driver was friendly. He chatted with us and said the children were probably five and eight years old, a girl and a boy. "They are with the mother," he said, "but their father is back in Mexico." Did he really believe that? The father was most likely already in the Unites States, in Oregon, Florida, or North Carolina. Who knows how long he'd been separated from his family? Since it has become so arduous and dangerous to cross back and forth across the border, circular migration has diminished. Now migrants come north for jobs and then send for their families. Many more women and children are coming now than in the past.

A Samaritan told of a woman who crossed with her eighteen-month-old son. The two were unable to keep up with the group, and, after much begging by the mother, the coyote agreed to take the toddler along. Then, in remorseful reconsideration, the mother went to the highway and flagged down the Border Patrol, weeping, and asked them to find her child. Meanwhile, the coyote had become impatient with the burden of the young niño and left him under a tree. The Border Patrol caught the coyote, who was able to recall the exact spot where the child had been left. The toddler was rescued.

The children you see crossing tug at your heart. The children who die break your heart. Just months ago a three-year-old child died of dehydration while crossing the Tohono O'odham Nation land. The young mother was trying to reach her husband in California. He had begged her to bring their young son to the United States so they could be reunited as a family. Now the child was dead. The grief-stricken mother was inconsolable and lashed out in anger at her husband, blaming him for the loss. Unsympathetic authorities considered charging the mother with child abuse. Fortunately the consulate, in compassionate intervention, was able to nullify such action.

Children crossing tug at your heart.

Children who die crossing break your heart.

Story Twenty-nine

It was the middle of May. In the fellowship hall of a Tucson church we sat around a table with containers full of food. A group of us had brought dishes for a potluck supper for the family of Juan de Jesús Rivera Cota. Juan's aunt, Gloria Michel Galaviz, had arrived from Los Angeles the day before to help with funeral arrangements and to act as liaison for the family of her teenaged nephew, a Mexican national shot by the Border Patrol on the land of the Tohono O'odham Nation.

Juan and four others had been in a truck driving north through the dusty, dry terrain. They were less than a mile from the international line when they spotted a Border Patrol vehicle on the roadside, partially concealed by mesquite trees and creosote bushes. They turned and sped south, headed home to Mexico. When they rounded a bend in the road they saw a Border Patrol vehicle blocking their escape. Juan was driving. He swerved to go around the vehicle and clipped the right front fender of the patrol car. The truck continued at high speed. As they topped a rise, another Border Patrol vehicle waited beside the road. Shots were fired. Juan was hit and mortally wounded. The others escaped. One youth, Eduardo, was hit in the left knee. Eduardo ran back into Mexico, and later received medical attention for the gunshot wound to his knee. Though he suffered crippling injuries, he was thankful to still be alive, he said as he told his story. The Border Patrol reported only one shot fired.

We were a somber group sitting around the supper table with the family: tía Gloria, her brother-in-law Cirilio Rivera, the father of the deceased, and another man who was a close family friend. Juan's body had not yet been released to the funeral home, but preparations needed to be made so they could take the body back to Sonoyta, the town in Sonora where his father lived and where Juan would be buried. Sonoyta is a Mexican border town with a reputation for drug trafficking and a lot of traffic from American tourists who pass through headed for the beach at Puerto Peñasco, fondly known as Rocky Point.

Aunt Gloria had flown in from Los Angeles two nights before to assist the family, both because of her English proficiency and because she is a legal U.S. resident. Riding in the taxi from the Tucson airport, she wept almost uncontrollably. She told us about the compassionate taxi driver who inquired if there was anything he could do to help. She told him the story. He knew of a friend's humanitarian work with the Samaritans organization, and he gave her a call.

The next day we were all involved. Discussing events around the dinner table, one of the attorneys said that we should have a representative of the family look at the body, someone who could reassure the family and who could verify that there were no unreported injuries. Suddenly a finger pointed in my face and an authoritative voice said, "Norma, you need to do the autopsy." I hadn't actually done an autopsy since my sophomore year in medical school. I did observe quite a few when I was practicing medical oncology, though. There were times, after the death of a patient, when I attended the postmortem examination because I had wanted to know how much residual cancer was there, or whether the cause of death was from the cancer itself or related to a complicating infection. But it was out of the question for me to do the postmortem exam on this casualty of our militarized border.

The attorney called the office of the Pima County Medical Examiner. The body was still in the county morgue and would be transferred to the funeral home later that day or the following morning. Permission was given for me to examine the body there.

The entryway into the funeral home the next morning was quiet and somber. Nothing moved. A few cars sat in the parking lot outside. In the low-lit room there was not one soul—or at least not one living person that I could see. The quietness and stillness calmed me. I almost tiptoed. It was another universe. Then someone came in to greet me. Subdued but professional, she told me she would inform the person in charge that I was waiting. It was a peaceful place to wait. Two women came into the office and beckoned me to follow. They knew I was coming and made me feel comfortable. I was not sure which of the young women was in charge, but both seemed informed and experienced. They were dressed in funereal black, and the one with pallid appearance, blonde hair pulled severely back from her face, could have been a member of the Addams Family. She showed very little expression, that same exotic presence as Anjelica Huston. She led the way to the room that contained the body. We paused outside as she pulled rubber gloves from a container beside the door, and each of us gloved up. The room was cold. Fortunately I had anticipated this and wore a cardigan sweater over my sleeveless blouse.

I walked into a scene that could have been from a crime show on television. In the center of the room was a stainless steel table on top of which lay a black vinyl bag the size of a human body. A zipper ran down the center of the bag. I guess we would see a lot more of these on TV news if the administration had not forbidden the televising of bodies being returned from Iraq. The Addams Family woman took charge and unzipped the bag. Out of the corner of my eye, I saw both women surreptitiously checking me out to see if I reacted. I remained expressionless.

The body on the table was just a kid. That day was his birthday. He would have been seventeen if he had lived one more day. His body was so bloated and discolored that I felt I was looking at an object. Maybe it was because the appearance was so lifeless that my emotions did not well up, or had I successfully prepared myself and locked my feelings in the car outside? Ms. Addams began pointing out things and giving explanations. I probed bullet holes with my gloved finger.

His left eye was massively swollen and purple. I raised the eyelid. The eyeball was intact, the swelling behind the eye and the periorbital tissues. There were two holes in the skull. Were they gunshot wounds? That is what it looked like to me. The two women agreed. There was one hole just above the right eyebrow and a second above the right ear, each hole a different size. The two women, also not forensic pathologists, but certainly more experienced than I at seeing gunshot wounds, expressed the opinion that these wounds were not from a shotgun but a more powerful weapon. I examined the interior of the skull and found no evidence of an exit wound. Maybe one of the bullets exited the left eye—but the eyeball was intact. Maybe it had lodged in the brain, which had been removed. Or maybe it had rolled around in the left eye socket, which was why there was so much swelling, and then fell out when the brain was removed. The Border Patrol had reported only one shot was fired.

In the left upper arm there were two holes in the soft tissue. This seemed consistent with gunshot wound entrance and exit sites. On examination of the right forearm, just proximal to the wrist, there was a single hole of a smaller caliber than that in the left upper arm. From that wound there was an incision that extended up to the elbow. The incision has been sutured. I decided that it was a postmortem incision done to search for the bullet, which went into the wrist and must have rico-cheted off the bone and upward toward the elbow and lodged there.

The abdomen was very distended and discolored, with a great deal of ecchymoses over the surface. Ms. Addams took my hand and rubbed it across the abdominal surface to demonstrate the crepitance in the tissues. Crepitance is a sound or feeling of a crackling sensation in the tissues. It can be caused by different pathological conditions: one example is the crunching sound you here in a creaky joint. In this case the abdominal wall was swollen, and there was air in the tissues of the abdominal wall itself, tiny pockets that had formed in the fat tissue. The cause of this was infection. As my hand stroked across the stomach using a little pressure I could feel a sort of crunchy or crackling feeling, sort of like a Rice Krispies sound. This condition probably occurred postmortem and was due to the breakdown of the tissues and gas-producing bacteria from the colon that infiltrated the dead tissues—the type of bacteria that causes gangrene.

The chest, back, and legs were negative for pathological findings. On the right side of the neck were several sutures. I thought this was done in the hospital, not in the morgue, and most likely was the site of an intravenous catheter or other medical device for monitoring his physiological status while in the intensive care unit, where he had been for several days. He wasn't disconnected from life support until the family was at the hospital.

Reporting on the funeral, the afternoon paper said that most of the mourners in attendance were volunteers from humanitarian groups in Tucson and southern Arizona in addition to pallbearers and officiating clergy. Following the service, we planned to accompany the hearse transporting Juan's body to Sonoyta, Mexico, the home of his father. The Mexican consulate had paid for all expenses of funeral preparations. But there was no provision to cover the cost of transporting his body back to his hometown on the Mexico–Arizona border; so when the funeral was over, Juan's casket was placed in the back of a Samaritan's truck, and the funeral procession inched away from church property. Out Highway 86 we proceeded, led by the rusted, yellow truck, passing through the Tohono O'odham Nation land toward Sonoyta.

Two Samaritans rode in the lead vehicle that carried the casket, and following behind was the red Saturn station wagon with bumper stick-ers proclaiming "Veterans for Peace," "Iraq—NO," and "Pro Choice, Pro Child." The driver, a retired physician, was a faithful Samaritan and compassionate activist. His passenger was Señor Rivera, the father of the dead teenager. When the procession made a rest stop at a gas station, Sr. Rivera got out of the car and went over to the truck. He raised the door of the camper shell and leaned in with hands on the casket, talking to his son.

Previous page: Image of Virgin of Guadalupe painted on rock wall near Nogales, Sonora.

Story Thirty

You might not even notice it. An ordinary shrub with a potent name—ironwood tree. Its wood is so dense it cannot float in water. But there is no water to be seen. Surrounded by low rocky mountains, the valley spreads in all directions. The vast floor is covered with varying sizes of ironwood, punctuated by cholla and towering saguaro. Like the gray-green clouds above, a canopy of ironwood covers what lies beneath.

As the desert formed, ironwood evolved ten million years ago and more, a time distance so large it makes no sense. In Ironwood Forest National Monument west of Tucson, two hundred Paleoindian archeological sites have been uncovered. Some trees are known to be eight hundred years old. Ironwood is the consummate hostess. As a nurse plant, it provides what is needed for over six hundred species to exist. Bighorn sheep, migrating birds, bats, iguanas, and millions and millions of fragile seeds owe their daily comings and goings to the protective roof of the ironwood.

We disrupt the ancient way of the desert by blasting off a man's fingers with an AK-47 and leaving a teenager dead in the cab of a truck in the darkness of three in the morning.

Yellow-and-black crime-scene tape saying "Do Not Cross This Line" in Spanish and English circumscribes fifty square yards of solitary desert, an hour's drive from human activity. We see coyote scat inside the taped area. Tire tracks bore through the sand, flattening prickly pear, agave, and cholla, coming to an abrupt halt near creosote bushes. On the ground lie shards of windshield glass next to a large brown spot where blood has poured from a pumping heart.

In the quiet early morning, a Dodge truck carrying ten migrants had crossed out of the Tohono O'odham Nation when four men following in another truck opened fire on the migrants. They shot off the fingers of the driver and shot a twenty-nine-year-old Guatemalan man, who died at the scene. Still alive were a Guatemalan woman with a gunshot wound in her neck and a fifteen-year-old girl. The assailants kidnapped the other migrants. Ten miles away, the police found an abandoned truck. In the cab were two people, shot to death, an eighteen-year-old man and a forty-year-old woman, both Mexicans.

We gather for a memorial service, a group of thirty. From the dirt road, we step across the yellow tape and walk to the dried blood near the creosote. I am a stranger to the kingdom of violence, but not to the desert. The blood is at once shocking and natural. The desert knows blood. It knows death and birth. It knows order.

But what is confusing are the navy-blue high heels. It is the first hint that we don't belong. She can't navigate the stones. I wonder if a person who has to concentrate on walking can, at the same time, focus on making sense? As she begins to do her standup again, the television reporter's sharp high heels sink into the soil. She is here to report, to explain what happened, who were the killers, who was killed, and why. She is here to make sense. She is not of this place.

We have all come to make sense, come to superimpose our clean, compartmentalized world on a morning of horror. We have come to make things solid, to ward off the certainty that we are as transient as migrants or birds. We stand here, intruders. We come to mourn. We bring with us our human ritual and television crew. We want to explain murder. We wonder what long line of international political folly and personal cravings brought us to this tragedy. The minister tells us that a reward is offered to anyone who knows about the crime. We will figure it out. There will be order.

Nearby, an eight-hundred-year-old ironwood waits.

Story Thirty-one

We are smack in the center of the days of death. Even though I have experienced this heat every summer of my life, it is always a shock. I step out of the cool car into the white-hot heat. It is the moment that begins to unravel the thread from comfort to alarm. Heavy heat wraps around, like too many blankets. It begins cooking from the outside, heating the epidermal layer of skin, while simultaneously warming you from the inside. Moisture starts to leave the skin until it feels equally hot inside and outside. Under my straw hat, I feel heat and pressure like the buildup of afternoon thunderstorms, and then the trickle of sweat starts down my temples. The base of my neck grows damp. It is like putting on a wet suit to hike the desert. And all this while standing still.

Every inch of my body is covered with clothing except my hands. Later, as I hike, the backs of my hands will burn. I will turn my hand so the back is hiding against my pant legs, turning the palm to the sun. When that burns beyond endurance, I will turn the hand again. Flip-flopping until finally I have to leave them in my pockets.

Three of us walk over to the cow graveyard, a hundred square yards of flat desert with remains of a few animals on it. One steer carcass is on the ground, the dark hide covering the skeleton like a blanket laid gently over the memory of a breathing creature. The soft spot under the tail, the eyes and the nostrils, eaten. There is a pile of dirt as tall as we are, with incandescent white femur bones sticking up, half-buried. It must be where cowboys dragged dead cattle and covered them up because of flies. Only they aren't covered.

Later, we would drive onto a ranch road. We drove slowly, looking for the road to public land near the mountains. A cowboy ran toward us, brandishing a rolled-up lasso. He jumped the fence, landing in front of the truck.

"What are you doing?"

"Going over to those mountains."

"Not on this road, you're not." His eyes were flat and his mouth barely opened when he spoke.

"But I've been this way before. I had permission," said the driver.

"Who gave it to you?"

"A ranch hand from here."

"That won't work." Eyes even flatter.

We turned around and drove to the ranch house. Our female driver walked to the door. A woman opened the door but stayed in the shadow behind the screen.

"We just want to cross your property to get back to the mountains."

"The ranch is closed."

"We can't cross here?"

"Closed from March through September."

"Why?"

"Vandalism."

Our friend asked the woman a few more questions, but the woman had quit speaking. Finally our friend came back to the car, followed by the other woman, who stopped and stared at us three very white gringas. I was sitting in the back seat, trying to look even more Anglo because we heard that brown-skinned people were not welcome at some of these ranches and that they might get shot. She didn't even invite us in for a beer.

Don't they have vandalism any other time of year? March through September. Those are the months of soaring migrant deaths. But maybe this rancher is just a very private person and understandably doesn't want strangers on her land. Or maybe they have something to hide here. Maybe the ranchers have witnessed some of these deaths. In April, Minutemen were given permission to be on this property twenty-four hours a day for thirty days. Or maybe the *polleros* pay the ranch hands for safe passage. Who knows? The mind tends to run toward suspicion when there is no friendly offer of beverages in the desert.

We backtracked on the ranch road to an area unfamiliar to us and started walking. Normally, sound describes what lies ahead, but there were no sounds except our breathing and walking. This was new territory for us. We kept hearing of migrant deaths in more and more remote areas. This was remote. The three of us walked in a line, even though there was no path. We followed the base of the mountain like a ship hugs the shoreline before moving out to sea. We thought maybe we would find migrants resting up for the evening walk and offer water, or in a real health emergency our doctor would know how to handle it.

There was no life—not a lizard, spider, scorpion, no birds. Just the tough desert vegetation that I kept snagging my pants on. My dad called them "espérate" bushes, wait-a-minute bushes. We saw scraggly mesquites, short brown clumps of grass and cholla forests that people navigated at night. Then we heard a noise that we couldn't figure out. Extreme heat alters sound. We came upon a fan-shaped concrete slab. At first we thought it was a helicopter landing pad. But it slanted down slightly, and at the base was a five-foot-tall column of yellow jackets, the only living thing we were to see on the day's patrol. They were droning above a two-foot-square cistern in the ground, full of thick green slime. I thought if I were dying of thirst, I would battle those yellow jackets for that wet green and would probably lose on both counts. I would have been stung beyond recognition and then vomited from the hot sludge I'd swallowed. Welcome to the desert.

In the white noon were distant mountains, the arroyo fanning ahead, palo verde trees, our faces, our eyebrows, all the color of chalk. Even what should have been green was bleached yellow. Covered with dust, we moved through the pale landscape like a ghost search-party looking for the already dead.

We spotted a cap, then a backpack, then the dust-covered camp. Clothing folded, pants on top of jackets. Gloves. Winter gear. The hard creases in the shirts indicated that these things had been here a long time, at least since last winter, possibly the winter before. Wool masks to keep the face warm on a cold night. Big blue five-gallon water containers, empty. Single-gallon jugs full of water the color of baby poop. We emptied those. Backpacks with rock-hard limes inside. Toothpaste tubes with tiny nibbles lacing the edges like embroidery where a rodent had feasted. Toothpaste tubes split open with hard pieces of toothpaste parted like chunks of ice broken off from arctic floes.

And beyond that one, another camp. Then another and another. Why did the people leave all their belongings here? They usually discard everything near a road where they will be picked up in a vehicle to begin the next phase of their journey. But there were no roads we could see. Why did they leave? Where did they go? We were miles from a road. Maybe a helicopter spotted them and sent in Border Patrol agents on horseback; maybe ranchers came in and rounded them up; maybe the Minutemen came in to play war.

Migrant belongings left at pickup site.

For some reason, I kept thinking about Miguel while we walked. I think this is the kind of terrain he walked through. Last June, two other volunteers and I were driving Arivaca Road laughing and singing loud with the radio. I know when things happen they happen fast, but we hadn't seen anyone for two days, so we were relaxed. We came sailing around a corner and passed them. We turned around. They were on the south side of the road. One standing, one lying down. The one standing called, "Can you help us? We're lost, we've been walking five days. My friend here is very sick." We jumped out of the car.

"What's his name?" I asked.

"Miguel."

Miguel was on his back on the ground, his face in sparse shade from a mesquite. Two of us knelt beside him. He was breathing but barely moving. The other volunteer went to get water and supplies from the car.

I had never seen anyone so skinny. Miguel was a little over five feet tall, possibly ninety pounds. We could see bones in front of his temple, and his cheekbones were sharp to the touch.

"Miguel, how are you? Miguel, can you hear me?"

No response.

"What is your name?" I asked him. He tried to lift his head but dropped it back down. He was burning up. It was 110 degrees in the atmosphere, probably 120 on the ground. As we put a little water on his tongue, ice under his armpits and on his groin, we kept talking to him.

"Miguel, where are you from? Talk to us, Miguel."

We got him to sit up a little and swallow some water. He wasn't sweating, a bad sign. He could get to his elbows but then fell back. There was no time to chat about this one. "Let's take him in." We put his arms over our shoulders, and Luis, the friend, helped get him in the car. Luis was limping from blisters covering the mound of the foot, we discovered later. Luis told us they had just left seven women from Honduras who were also lost.

I drove. The woman beside me called the hospital, doctor, and lawyer to let everyone know we were on the way with a patient, as was our protocol at that time. The other volunteer was in the backseat putting ice on Miguel's forehead.

We walked into the emergency room. Miguel had one arm draped over each of our shoulders, his head bobbing forward. We were almost dragging him. One of the angels behind the desk said, "Samaritans?" We said yes, and she rushed out to help us into triage. As she was taking his vital signs, he whispered that he was going to die and gave me his daughter's name and a phone number in a village, but we couldn't hear him, his voice was so weak. I had a terrible feeling. They rushed him behind a curtain and inserted an IV. He didn't respond much. His narrow dark face was like a skull, and there seemed to be no liquid under his skin. I was worried about his kidneys. His wrists were like a little girl's. He was forty years old. After a while, they gave another IV. He started to cry. He said he didn't want to die. We assured him he wouldn't. He started to talk, but we had to lean over the bed to hear.

He said he had been traveling a month in Mexico, working as he traveled, trying to get enough money to cross. He said he had a woman, and two daughters from a different marriage, and they would be sad if he died but should know if it happened. He told us he was on the desert five days, that there were things worse than death. That he had walked past *un esqueleto*, a skeleton, one day and a second skeleton on another day. One had a hand sticking out of the ground with skin still on it. There are things worse than death, he said again, and sobbed.

Miguel lived, thanks to the nurses. But we never found the seven Honduran women.

Men apprehended by Border Patrol at Amado, Arizona.

Border Patrol transfers detainees to Homeland Security bus.

Story Thirty-two

If it had gone another way, it would have been a normal day. We would have helped some people and moved on. But it turned out differently.

Just past the bridge on Arivaca Road, we pulled over to take a short break. We were three Samaritans in a four-wheel-drive Rodeo. It was noon, and we had been searching for people in distress since 6:00 a.m. We were standing by the car talking, a photojournalist, a filmmaker, and I.

Another Samaritan patrol saw us and pulled up to visit. Four women got out of the car. We talked, stretched, walked around a little. We were about forty feet from a small bridge. Big cottonwoods crowded up to the side of the road, hanging over the dry wash that funneled under the small, low bridge. The bridge was just high enough for water to pass under with no extra breathing room. It was a 105-degree day in June. There had been no rain for weeks and none in the forecast.

As we were talking, the filmmaker walked over to the trees. I turned a few minutes later and saw his eyes light up, pointing toward the bridge and silently mouthing the word "migrants."

If it had gone another way, it would have been a normal day. I would have grabbed the blister bag and my backpack and run to the bridge.

If it had been a normal day, I would have crawled under the bridge with the four migrants and started asking if they needed water, were they ill, did they have blisters, sprained ankles, cuts, were they diabetic, any heart conditions. I would have checked Antonio's feet as he sat against the inside wall, his head touching the top of the bridge. I would have washed his feet to begin treating the enormous blister, banging my head on the ceiling of the low bridge.

Antonio would have told me that he had no sons, only a daughter. That he loved his seven-year-old daughter, Lara. That on his day off, his wife would start the afternoon meal while he and Lara headed for the arroyo that ran along the edge of town, past the road to the cathedral. She would put her hand in his as he guided her down the trail into the wash looking for damp sand to walk on. They would smell decay from the layers of cottonwood leaves. Lara would run through the leaves, up the huge gnarled cottonwood roots, climbing over roots and fallen branches. And he would tell me how they would sit under their favorite tree and watch the Great Owl sleep high up on the top branch.

And he would tell me how he could no longer sit with his daughter and wait for the owl's night cries, how he could no longer splash in the cool stream with her, and how he could no longer dream of dropping stars into his daughter's lap.

He could no longer dream. He had come north to work. He could only think of tonight's walk, how sweat will drip down his back even though it is night. How he brought the garlic strand he wears around his neck to keep scorpions away, how he is afraid of rattlesnakes, afraid of spraining an ankle on a rock in the dark, afraid of the footsteps he hears behind him, footsteps with no face, no moonlight to reflect the glint of eyes or the glint of a razor-sharp weapon, footsteps of bandits or Border Patrol. How he has to think one step at a time, one mile at a time for 160 more until they reach Phoenix.

If it had been a normal day, I would have reached over and handed a food pack to eighteen-year-old Rodolfo. He would have grinned and said in English, "You roke, lady." And he would have handed a pack to his sixteen-year-old brother, Ramon, who wore a black Virgin of Guadalupe T-shirt, the image of the Virgin filling the entire shirt, the pointed red and green rays covering his chest like a suit of armor. Both brothers would wear their Chicago Cubs baseball caps pointing sideways.

And Rodolfo would have told me in rapid-fire Spanish how they were going to Oregon to see the parents they hadn't seen in three years. That their parents came to the United States three years ago to work and finally saved enough money to send for the boys, who were living in Chihuahua. As soon as the boys got jobs, they were going to buy a radio for their parents. Back home, they had a radio with a coat hanger twisted on as an antenna and could get a station that played great music. Dad had strung a couple of light bulbs outside behind Grandmother's house. He would make carne asada, the whole family would be there, and Dad would grab Mom's waist and, one-two one-two, they would dance until the rooster crowed. "Está bien chido," it's cool, he would have said.

If it had been a normal day, Miguel, his back propped against the wall in the shade under the bridge, a silhouette against the ruthless sun a few inches beyond, would have opened his food pack and dived into the applesauce first. He would have quietly said thank you. He would have said nothing else, soberly listening to the others, keeping his dreams and fears tucked close against his heart, not to be shared.

But it had gone another way, and it was not a normal day. We did not help and then move on. Instead, all of us from the two vehicles were talking, relaxing, meandering across the road. The filmmaker saw the migrants hiding under the bridge, then he told me, and I told the others. We were surprised because there had been no hint they were there. From that moment on, everything we did was an instant too late. Everything went wrong. I asked someone to throw me the blister bag. It fell open to the ground, supplies falling out. We scurried to pick it up. I gave the keys to someone to drive. Instead of driving away, everyone started walking toward the bridge to help.

At that moment, a Border Patrol vehicle sped past. I saw his brakelights flash on a hundred yards up the road. He stopped. We didn't want to jeopardize the men under the bridge. The Samaritan ladies got in their vehicle; we got in ours. It was too late. The agent turned his truck around faster than I could imagine possible and was back beside us before our ignition turned over. He was on his radio, screeching to a stop across the road from us. He was shouting into his radio "Arivaca Road, Milepost 3, MP 3," opening his door while still calling in the information. The agent jumped out of his truck and picked up a walkie-talkie as he put his right hand on his pistol. He was moving away from us toward the wash on the other side of the road.

I have never been in a war but felt I was standing at the edge, watching one.

I looked over at the other side of the road and saw the four men running up the wash, sloshing through deep hot sand and rocks. They must have panicked and left the safety of the bridge. They looked over their shoulders, back toward the Border Patrol agent, faces broken with fear. I saw the Virgin of Guadalupe T-shirt and hoped the green and red rays were indeed armor. Struggling to run, one man threw down his backpack, another tripped but got up, and they all rounded the bend, out of my sight.

I looked at the agent's face. Beyond the glossy surface of the eye, deep inside, it was hard and angular—no soft edges or recognition that what he was about to chase was made of the same blood, skin, sinew, and soul as he. No recognition that he was hunting down his own species. The clean, steely precision of the military doesn't allow for the edgeless peculiarity of desire, empathy, or hope.

The agent ignored us, started running, hand reaching for his holstered gun. He mistook a dream for an enemy on two legs. The hunt was on. But the prey had no chance. The agent had called for backup. There is more Border Patrol backup than there are stars in the sky. Second only to dollars poured into Iraq and Afghanistan, Homeland Security receives more funding than any other U.S. agency.

I watched as four men were hunted down like animals. I didn't see the end. Did one of them trip and fall against barbed wire that raked across his eyeball? Was one shoved to the ground, his face filled with cholla cactus? Was he kicked in the stomach by a regulation boot?

If it had been a normal day, we would have helped and moved on. We didn't. We have since wondered if it was our fault they were captured. Were we too slow? Was it fate? Would it have happened anyway if we hadn't been there? We think about it again and again. If only.

Story Thirty-three

Tick-tick-tick. One second at a time. One thought at a time. Epifanio couldn't make it happen faster. He knew they should move, but it was so hot. He touched his wife's face. It burned. Marcela was sitting with her back against the trunk of a mesquite tree with her head back, eyes closed.

She was ill and could not keep the fast pace of the group. In the night, the others walked on, leaving Epifanio, his fourteen-year-old daughter, Mica, and his wife behind. He was hoping that when it got cooler, they could walk more. He had no idea where they were but thought they could continue following the trail north.

For seven years, they had tried to get a visa to come to the United States to visit grandchildren they had never seen. But after seven years, the web of government red tape was so dense that the visa still had not come through. The final solution was to cross the Arizona desert and connect with a ride to Tennessee.

Epifanio heard a noise . . . zzzz . . . like a swarm of bees. As it got louder, he knew it wasn't insects. He jumped up to move his family to the bushes, but it was too late. Two men on all-terrain vehicles came down the hill, a cloud of dust behind them, speeding toward Epifanio. He felt a wave of alarm. The men were not dressed to protect, they were dressed to kill.

They were wearing slate-gray uniforms, black gloves, and tall boots, their heads covered in black and gray helmets with smoky curved plates covering their faces. Epifanio could see no part of a human body. They wore heavy vests and were protected by knee and elbow pads, with low pockets on the legs full of heavy objects. On the belts hung pistols and mace.

"¡Papá!" cried Mica, who knelt beside her mother. Roaring through a wall of dust, the ATVs arrived. One circled the family. The other ATV stopped. A man jumped off, running toward them, shouting "¡Híncate!" Get on your knees. Epifanio knelt in the dirt. The man yelled, "¿Cual es su nacionalidad?" "What's your nationality?" Epifanio could see the Border Patrol emblem and the U.S. flag on his jacket. "¿Dónde están los otros?" "Where are the others?" "Se fueron." They left.

The agents called in on the radio. Epifanio could hear only part of what they said. He heard a voice say "bodies" in English. He thought that meant they were going to be killed. His heart raced.

Mica moved in front of her mother to protect her.

The agents spoke to each other in English but to Epifanio in Spanish. After more questions, one agent said "Levántense." Get up.

"My wife is sick. She can't walk," Epifanio said.

The agent walked to Epifanio and shouted at him to get moving.

Epifanio moved to his wife, kneeled, and said, "We have to go. Can you make it?" She stood. Mica grabbed her mom's arm. Epifanio picked up the backpacks, Mica's *lotería* lottery cards falling to the dirt. She looked back at the cards. She cried out "¡La Sirena!" The mermaid. She moved toward the cards. Her father took her by the hand and turned her forward. They began to walk.

The trail widened into flat sandy desert, no shade for miles. Epifanio asked an agent for water. The agent took a bottle out of his pack, drank, put it back in the pack. Driving close to Epifanio, he pushed the family forward with his ATV.

After an hour of forced walking, Marcela fell to the ground. One agent got off his ATV and told them to keep walking. Marcela lay on the ground, her face in the dirt. The other agent drove toward Marcela, veered close to her body, riding doughnuts around and around Marcela. He slowed, reversed, circled, decreasing the circumference of the circle with each turn. He smiled, satisfied with his ride.

He slid sideways over to the other agent. "Did you see that? I got this baby under control, bro! Handles almost like a dirt bike. I was bored a while ago, but this is turning out to be fun."

Epifanio ran to his wife and shouted for water. The agents ignored him. He kept shouting. Mica cried. The ATV rider said, "These guys are gonna be a problem. Let's leave 'em here and get back."

The other agent said, "We can't, they'll die."

The first agent said, "That's not our problem. We didn't tell 'em to come here."

Not knowing that Epifanio spoke English, they continued their discussion, then left, leaving the family with no water.

Marcela lay on the ground with her arm over her face. Epifanio placed his body so it shaded her. His body vibrated with anger, but there was nothing more to do. Mica sat nearby, crying. Finally, Epifanio lay down on his back. His ribcage expanded and fell back in on itself. There was a pressure on his chest. The heat sat on him like a grizzly, suffocating him.

He had nothing with which to help his wife. He was an educated man with his own practice as a naturopath in Cuernavaca, Mexico. His job was to heal, but now he was helpless. All he could do was talk to her, tell her to stay with him.

An hour later, a white pickup truck drove up to them. The man driving wore a white cowboy hat, his companion a red ball cap. There was a rifle in the gunrack of the cab. They gave the family water, then called an ambulance and drove the family to the east side of Highway 286, across from Baboquivari Mountain, to wait. The medics came with Border Patrol. The agents separated the family, sending Marcela to Tucson in the ambulance and putting Epifanio and Mica in the back of an unventilated vehicle.

The Border Patrol agents got in the cab. From inside the compartment, Epifanio and Mica could see light through a single window on the rear door. The small window had mesh wire between the panes of glass. Epifanio was tall, so he had to bend forward on the bench to keep from hitting his head. The cramped vehicle was more accommodating if you were on all fours, but it smelled like vomit.

Mica held her father's hand. They drove another half hour. Then Mica and Epifanio were transferred to a bus with other migrants and driven to a detention center in Tucson.

Marcela was near death. She had adrenal insufficiency and was placed in the hospital ICU. Epifanio, in detention, was outraged. No one would tell him where his wife was or what had happened. He demanded information and received none. He was sick to his stomach from worry and hunger. He ladled water from a communal bucket to give to Mica, who drank in small sips.

Marcela's eyes adjusted to the light in the hospital room. "Where's my daughter? Where's my husband?" she asked. The nurses busied themselves and didn't answer. Marcela tried to stay awake but drifted off under medication.

On the third night at the Border Patrol detention center, around midnight, an agent came in and told Epifanio they were taking him to the hospital because his wife was gravely ill.

Epifanio sat with Marcela all night. Mica sat close to her mom. She would start to fall asleep but would suddenly wake, then move her chair closer and lay her head on the blanket, trying to curl up with her mom without climbing onto her bed.

In a rare stroke of empathy, or perhaps because Epifanio had contacted the Mexican consulate in Tucson, the authorities gave the family an eight-day field release, also known as a compassionate visa, allowing them to stay in the United States a little longer.

Not long afterward, George W. Bush, president of the United States, declared that no more compassionate visas would be given.

Marcela improved slightly. On the seventh day she was transferred out of the ICU into a regular room, still not well. On the eighth day, she, Mica, and Epifanio were standing in the hospital parking lot with no money, no medicines, no contacts, in a town they had never heard of.

Norma

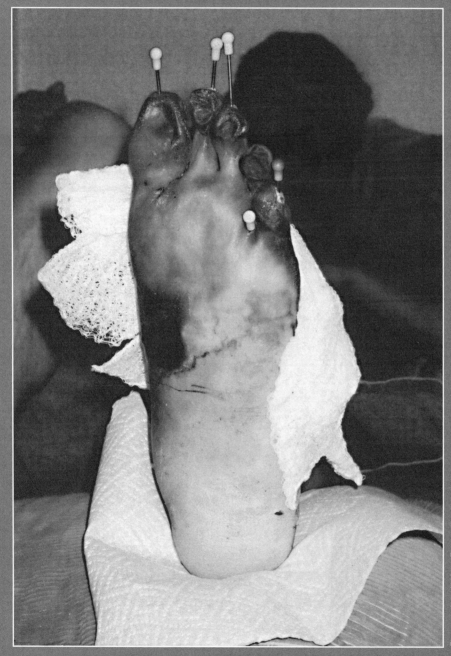

Photograph by Kathryn Ferguson

Previous page: Foot mangled from train injury.

Story Thirty-four

Benjamin Hill is the name not of a Spanish-speaking migrant but of a simple little pueblo ninety miles south of the Arizona-Mexico border. It is a place where trains and migrants rendezvous. Here in this community, with only a few paved streets, no stoplight, and three churches, freight trains from southern Mexico arrive full of cargo inside and migrants on top. In this village they change to trains headed west to Mexicali or north to Nogales, two border towns, one on the California-Mexico border and one on the Arizona-Mexico border. The migrants arrive in large clusters, stuck to the tops, the sides, even underneath boxcars. When they reach the village of Benjamin Hill, they camp in the large fields beside the railroad tracks, awaiting freight trains headed for the border. At one of the two Catholic churches in town, the migrants can have a substantial meal before the trains leave at 10:30 a.m. Doña Alicia is the *jefa* in charge of the breakfast program. On busy days she and some of her fellow parishioners feed 120 migrants or more, mostly men. Alicia began this mission after she had a dream, "a vision." Jesus Christ appeared to her and told her to feed the poor, to help the migrants passing through town, changing trains, heading north for jobs. Moved and inspired by her vision, she gathered the women in the church and community and started the breakfast program.

Several blocks from the church, the main street turns and crosses the railroad tracks to another neighborhood. Just beyond the turn, on the other side of the gully, is a large field with a few trees. Scattered figures in dark clothes can be seen leaning against the trees. This field will be bed for the migrants tonight. There are several trains along the tracks, all of them still right now. On the other side of the railroad are neat houses with flowers and a few trees in the yards. Here is the other church, in the midst of the nicer homes. There is a school and

playground right next to the lovely, white sanctuary. Padre Quiñones's living quarters are here. There is a large kitchen, well supplied,
that serves lunches to schoolchildren and the less fortunate citizens of
Benjamin Hill. Several times Padre Quiñones has invited us into the
modest entry room of his living quarters. On the wall hangs a large portrait of Pope John Paul II. I always remember Padre Quiñones as a tall,
large, bearlike man. But he is tall not in stature but in spirit.

On one occasion, Tucson clergyman John Fife went with another
Samaritan and me down to Benjamin Hill to take provisions to Señora
Alicia for the breakfast program, and we met Padre Quiñones for lunch.
When I saw the two great men of God and of the people embrace, laugh,
and toss false accusations and jokes at each other, I knew their spirits
filled a void in this world.

During the Sanctuary movement of the 1980s, Padre Quiñones
was one of two Mexican nationals indicted by the U.S. government
as a conspirator to transport illegal immigrants from Central America. Because he was Mexican, he had no responsibility to appear in the
U.S. court, but every day for six months he drove the ninety kilometers from Nogales to Tucson to appear in court alongside the other ten
defendants. At that time, over twenty years ago, he was a priest in that
city on the Mexican border. When tortured, threatened, and persecuted
Central Americans came through Mexico, headed for the United States
to request asylum, they sought temporary refuge in Nogales. Padre
Quiñones had his parishioners leave their photo ID border passes at the
church. When the Central Americans arrived in Nogales, they would
sort through the photo IDs until one of similar appearance to the refugee was found. Then the asylum seeker crossed the border and was
picked up by a Sanctuary worker and sent on the way to a safer locale.
The ID was then sent back to Nogales, Sonora, to be used again when
a match was appropriate or when the rightful owner of the ID needed
to cross the border.

Pastor John Fife and Padre Ramón Dagoberto Quiñones were truly
soul brothers. They shared an unspoken closeness, forged in a battle
that thrust them into the public eye, but that few outside of battlefield
brotherhood will ever experience.

Every few months we visited Benjamin Hill to take food provisions
and as many shoes and socks as we could accumulate through dona-
tions. The tired travelers were always grateful for contributions. Many
times the soles of their shoes were completely worn through, and I sus-
pect their souls were worn through also.

Eight of us sat outside in front of the entrance of la Iglesia Mila-grosa, discussing improvements to the kitchen and eating area. Along with five other volunteers, I had come again to Benjamin Hill to meet with Señora Alicia and Padre Quiñones and decide how to implement repairs to the area where breakfast is served to migrants six days a week. The floor is dirt. Flaking plaster and peeling paint cover one wall of the space flanked by the church on one side and a store on the other. The sink where they wash dishes is shallow, and the lack of any counter space cramps the work of the women who prepare and serve. As we talked, I strained to follow the discussion, since of the group I was the least fluent in Spanish. I faced the front of the church with my back toward the street; Brent, one of the volunteers, sat across from me fac-ing the street. Padre Quiñones and we four women had been doing most of the talking. I don't think Brent had spoken at all. Now he looked toward me and nodded, his gaze directed at something behind me. He mouthed the words, "He needs you."

I turned and saw two bedraggled men in dirt-encrusted clothes crossing the dusty street. The one in front limped significantly and had a large white bandage on his right foot and a rubber thong sandal tied around the foot. On his left foot also was a rubber thong sandal. Did he walk through the desert in those? The two passed by, headed toward the eating area. When there was a lull in the discussion about building improvements, I slipped away to check on the patient. Moises inquired if I needed help, and I asked him to please come in case I needed help with translation.

The two bedraggled men ate tortillas with bowls of *fideo* soup, a rich broth with noodles. "¿Cómo está?" I asked. "¿Le duele su pie?" I looked down and saw very clearly that the right foot was shorter than the unbandaged left foot. I did not even need to ask what his problem was. I told him to finish eating and then I would examine his foot. "Soy doctora," I explained. He then told me what had happened. He was hop-ping trains, and he slipped, and his foot was caught between two train cars while they were being hitched together. His toes and the distal part of his foot were severed. When the train reached its destination, there was an ambulance waiting that took him to the hospital in Los Mochis.

The man with him wore a black T-shirt bearing the logo of a rock band, and a long cord with two medals dangled down the front of his shirt. His black hair hung below his ears, accentuating the gaunt-ness of his face. I turned to him and asked, "Are you his brother or friend?" He replied that he was taking care of this man, an injured fel-low *campesino*.

"¿Cómo se llama?" I asked the injured man.

"Peter," he said.

I wrinkled my brow quizzically. "Pedro?" He nodded. He didn't speak very clearly, and most of what he said I could barely understand.

He was traveling from his home in the state of Chihuahua to the border town of Mexicali, where he hoped to find work. Part of the year he worked construction in Mexicali, and the rest of the year he worked in Chihuahua picking apples. His dream had been to go to Washington State to pick apples. There were no living relatives in Chihuahua. His mother died from systemic infection, complications of extensive burns over her torso that had become secondarily infected. One sister died of AIDS; another died in childbirth.

Brent helped get the meager supplies ready to bandage Peter's foot. Brent had spent time volunteering here in Benjamin Hill during the summer and had a lot of experience treating foot problems—everything from mild and bad blisters to fungal foot infections caused from wearing the same socks and shoes for three to four weeks, often sloshing through rain and mud. Brent told me there was water and a hose on one side of the church. I got a large pan to soak feet, and he went in search of bandage materials. While Brent searched for supplies, we asked Peter where he was from. He told us he was Tarahumara, one of the people who call themselves the Rarámuri, an indigenous population isolated in the Copper Canyon region in the state of Chihuahua. We rarely encounter any of this population among the migrants we see in the southern Arizona desert. They are such an isolated population and independent of any outside influence. In fact, I am not aware of any encounters with Tarahumara by volunteer groups. My fellow Samaritan Kathryn said that at one of the migrant campsites she had found a woven belt unique to the Tarahumara dress, but she was not aware of any encounters with Rarámuri people either.

Peter sat in a chair in the shade of a palm tree and started to unwrap the bandage on his foot. I spread a plastic bag on the ground for him to put his right foot on and next to it a pan of water to soak his left foot. He said that they had done surgery on his foot in the hospital in Los Mochis. He showed us the plastic bag of bandage supplies that had been given to him when he was discharged. There was a plastic cola bottle half full of iodine, sterile gauze pads individually wrapped, a tube of antibiotic ointment, and some medicine for pain. I decided to use whatever materials we had and not deplete his bandage supply. He began unwrapping the gauze from his foot. The bandage was charcoal gray with dust, dirt, and grime from walking in unpaved, dirt streets.

There were no gloves in our meager medical supplies, and while he soaked his left foot I wrapped plastic grocery bags around my hands, pulling plastic down between my fingers to fashion a sort of glove. I surveyed the gauze and looked for tape as I prepared to clean his foot and debride it if necessary.

Pedro finished unwrapping the dirty gauze from his foot. On the inside of the bandage was yellowish drainage. The bandage looked pretty awful, but the foot itself didn't look so bad—at least it didn't look infected, and there was no odor to suggest bacterial infection. No skin covered the stump of his foot. The area of exposed muscle tissue was shaped like a triangle pointing at the base of the tibia, the large bone of the lower leg. There was skin on the lateral and medial side of the foot. Only on the dorsum of the foot could you see muscle tissue. Some kind of yellowish-white gunk showed through in two spots. It wasn't pus but fascia, the fibrous tissue that encases muscle tissue. Several sutures dangled loose on the distal portion of the stump, right where the little toe should be, and another medially where the great toe would have connected. I cleaned the wound, put nonstick gauze pads over that portion of the foot, and in the absence of any rolled gauze I put a surgical mask over the bandage on the stump. It worked nicely since the masks are pleated and curved to fit. We took a thin pair of socks, cut off the top, and used the toe half to hold the dressing in place. Then he put on a pair of thick, absorbent socks. One sock over the dressing on the stump of the right foot and on his left foot he put the clean white sock with the thong sandal pulled between his toes.

I had difficulty understanding Peter, more than with some other Spanish speakers. I attributed this to Spanish not being his first language, if indeed his mother tongue was the indigenous Tarahumara language. When we drove back toward the border, Moises pointed out that Peter had flecks of paint in his hair. The fluent Spanish speakers also had noticed the slurring of his words. Maybe he had been sniffing paint or paint thinner. Was it for pain relief? Was it the trauma of his experience? Was it habitual? Maybe that is why he lost his grip and fell, losing his foot. Those street-smart in the ways of migrant travel say that the ones who ride the train stay high or drunk. Some places on the train are more desirable to sit, lie, or ride. These positions are fought over, and it is easier, they say, to fight for your place if you are drunk or drugged.

I looked at the two medals hanging from the neck of the man with Peter. One was a young girl's photo, maybe his daughter. The other was an image of Malverde, the patron saint of bandits and drug smugglers.

I hoped that Malverde or some other saint would watch over them as they continued on to Mexicali to look for jobs.

We rebandaged Peter's foot. Brent found an old broom handle and fashioned it into a cane for Peter to use for support and balance. As the two men headed back toward the railroad tracks, they turned and waved, saying thanks. My heart was heavy, but I knew they had not needed our help on their journey thus far. They would surely be able to survive and make their way as they continued their travel. Perhaps in Mexicali Peter would connect with humanitarian efforts from local people, and his friend could get the construction job he wanted.

Story Thirty-five

I had been told that Enrique, the man I was about to see, had lacerations on his face and eyelid, but still I was caught off guard. When Enrique looked directly at me, his face was lopsided and distorted with swelling. The right eyelid was swollen and his right eye protruded, bulging out like a Cyclops eye. For a split second I was taken back decades to the Baptist Hospital in Jackson, Mississippi.

It was the summer of my sixteenth year, and I had a job working at the hospital. I passed out magazines and helped patients with phone calls and letters, nothing that involved medical care, but every day I saw and talked with patients. That was the nidus of my medical career. The only patient that I remember from that summer was a young boy about six or seven years old who had an eye tumor. In my memory his deformity looked a lot like Enrique's. In retrospect I wonder if the boy's eye tumor wasn't a retinoblastoma, one of the childhood cancers. He had previously been treated with surgery and radiation therapy, but there had been a recurrence of the cancer, with massive, disfiguring swelling of his eye and of the entire side of his face. It was one of those times when you freeze the look on your face so as not to embarrass the boy or to make him feel in any way uncomfortable—so that he wouldn't know how uncomfortable you were. Just for a moment I felt that way when I saw Enrique.

"¿Que pasó?" I wanted to know how his injury occurred. As he began talking, I relaxed.

He told how he was injured when he tripped over a log in the dark and fell facedown onto barbed wire. As we talked, I examined the lacerations. I asked if he had contacted his family. "Sí," he said, and added that he was very relieved after speaking with Horacio, his twelve-year-old son back home in Michoacán, the state adjacent to the state of Mexico and west of Mexico City. It is a very scenic area with picturesque towns and the location of the El Rosario monarch butterfly sanctuary. A few years ago I visited the quaint and lovely colonial town of Pátzcuaro in Michoacán. People living there told me that in some of the villages around Lake Pátzcuaro there were no young men. The pueblos were populated by women, children, and the old. All the young and strong men had gone to the United States to work.

The night he was injured, Enrique was crossing the Tohono O'odham Nation's land with two companions, his brother and a friend. There was only a quarter moon in the sky. Usually, here in southern Arizona, the air is so clear and humidity so low that if there is a half moon or larger it is bright enough outside to see your shadow. But not that night. The friend knew some of the trails that migrants followed, but Enrique denied that his friend was a coyote—probably true, since I doubt a coyote would guide only two people unless they were well off and paid him the fare of twenty. After he fell, the other two men went with him to the highway to wait for Border Patrol or any passerby who would take him for medical help. The two *compañeros* waited across the road, hidden, until Border Patrol stopped. Once they were sure Enrique was taken care of, the two continued north on their journey.

The Border Patrol called for an ambulance, which took him to the Sells hospital. The Tohono O'odham land is almost the size of the state of Connecticut. The hospital there, run by Indian Health Service, treats many border crossers who become sick or injured when their journey takes them across that vast desert country. But there was no ophthalmology consultant available at the hospital that night, so after a long wait Enrique was transferred to a hospital in Tucson.

It had been two days since his injury, and he said he did not have much residual pain. I examined the laceration that extended across his forehead and upper right eyelid. It began above his left eyebrow, angled downward diagonally across his eye, and stopped in front of his right ear. The right eyelid was sutured. Steri-Strips, small pieces of reinforced tape, substitutions for sutures, held together the laceration on his forehead. There were a few other small cuts on his face where no closure was necessary, and a very nasty cut on the bridge of his nose that had crusted over with dried, black blood. Dried blood caked his eyelashes together, and a thick goo oozed out of his bulging right eye. This was the antibiotic ointment that he was applying to his eye daily, but it added to the discomfiting appearance.

The following day the swelling had decreased to half of what it had been. Now he was able to see the part of his eye that is supposed to be the "white of the eyes," and he was very worried because it wasn't. He asked, with great concern in his voice, about the *rojo* in his eye. There was extensive subconjunctival hemorrhage; so in the socket where his eye should have been was a ball of blood with a dark circle in the center. I knew that this would clear with time, and at that point the appearance was worse than the seriousness of the injury. I tried to reassure him. "Can you see OK?" I asked. "Sí," he replied. I cleaned the dried blood from the other lacerations and asked about his medications. Was he drinking enough water, and was he applying the ointment in his eye twice daily? It was his turn to reassure me with positive answers to my questions.

For several years Enrique had traveled back and forth between Mexico and the United States for work, never planning to stay here. He needed to earn more than was possible at home. He was very committed to his community. One of the reasons he came north to earn more money was that he wanted to support activities in his church. He and the fifty or so families who are members of the parish where he attended church were trying to accumulate enough money to renovate their house of worship. It was an old colonial church, beautiful but in need of much repair. Each of the families yearly gave fifty dollars to support the renovation. He wanted to contribute to the efforts of his congregation, he told me.

Every day, Enrique's facial lacerations improved and there was less swelling around his eye. He continued to be concerned about his vision and on questioning said that sometimes things looked a little blurry. I examined his eye again and explained that the blurriness was due to the ointment he was applying and would improve. He was relieved. While I doctored we talked with the help of a nurse and Samaritan who spoke fluent Spanish. Enrique told us more about his family and his previous stays in the United States. Six months ago he had worked construction in Florida, primarily as a roofer repairing hurricane-damaged houses. The contractor he worked for follows storms from one place to the next. When they left Florida, they went to Beaumont, Texas, to work. We asked if he had worked in New Orleans after Hurricane Katrina. He said no, they didn't need roofs—the whole city was flattened; they needed framers.

Back home there was only the one twelve-year-old son and a wife. Two years ago his sister was getting married in a nearby village in Michoacán, and there were seventeen relatives riding in a truck going to the wedding. A terrible accident occurred, and the rollover killed eight of the passengers, among them a sister, a sister-in-law, an eight-year-old nephew, and his own one-year-old son. Enrique's wife suffered fractured cervical vertebrae, and the doctor told her that if she moved her head the wrong way she could be paralyzed or might die. "Gracias a Dios," he said. She recovered completely. Enrique said that after that tragedy he got much closer to God. He tried to find meaning in his life and be more centered in a spiritual way. He felt that this injury also had purpose, testing and strengthening his faith.

When I last saw Enrique, the lacerations had healed nicely, and the only cut that might leave a scar was the jagged one on the bridge of his nose. Enrique was grateful that his vision wasn't affected and said he felt fortunate that the injuries were no worse. He expressed gratitude to us for our care, but credited his faith for sustaining him through his ordeal.

Group waiting for their guide.

Photograph by Helen Lundgren

Story Thirty-six

Luis was one of the commuters, a man who would have preferred to stay in his home country and work if he could have found employment, if he could have earned enough to support his family. In Guatemala, Luis made $2.50 a day. To do so, he traveled from his home to coffee plantations three days away.

We first saw Luis when we were on a Samaritan patrol in the remote Ironwood Forest National Monument northwest of Tucson. Ironwood is the northernmost route of our usual patrols, a desolate area. If someone were in trouble there, it is unlikely a casual passerby would find them in time to render aid. The forest is contiguous to the boundary of the land belonging to the Tohono O'odham Nation. Migrants crossing this land frequently wait for and meet their pickup ride at one of the rutted back roads of Ironwood Forest. There are campsites where migrants wait, and we find their discarded clothes, backpacks, and personal items. Several Humane Borders water stations are in the area. But it is a vast and empty area, and the roads require high-clearance vehicles, and some demand four-wheel drive.

That day on patrol we drove parallel to Indian land on a bumpy dirt road. We then continued on pavement till reaching the turn from Avra Valley Road onto Silverbell Road. We had seen no migrants and little evidence of their travels, only an occasional water jug or discarded backpack. We drove toward an old mine. Just before reaching the tailings, the road forked leading to the hamlet of Red Rock. Several years ago, five migrants were shot and killed while getting water from a cattle tank nearby. At the time, the shooting was attributed to drugs or violence between rival migrant smugglers, but the crime was never solved. Only four weeks ago a group of thirty or more of us stood between two ancient ironwood trees at a memorial service for three migrants shot and killed while crossing through Ironwood Forest. As the small group of humanitarians and representatives of the Guatemalan consulate gathered, someone stepped up and planted a small wooden cross next to a patch of brown sand where a puddle of blood had stained the desert floor. One by one, others stepped forward and placed rosaries, flowers, and a bouquet of branches from desert plants. Helen, one of the Samaritans, moved to protect the bloody scar on the desert floor, as she placed rocks outlining the umber stain. Others followed, and a small accumulation of inanimate desert witnesses surrounded the shrine, guarding the site of death and dashed hopes.

That day at the memorial service there was a feeling that it had been desecrated, those 129,000 acres of protected flora and environs. The day that we encountered Luis, there was not that feeling of stigma. The sun was bright, the day hot, and far ahead on the road we could see a bright yellow figure. As we got closer, that yellow blur took the shape of a person, a short person. Luis was standing on the shoulder of the road, several feet off the pavement, holding a bottle of water in one hand and a food bag in the other, the yellow soccer shirt hanging almost to his knees. A big grin on his face, white teeth framing a gap where two teeth were missing, and flashing black eyes disguised the pain of his severely blistered feet. It had been raining for several days, and his socks and shoes were soggy. The soles of his feet were covered with large puffy blisters roofed over by wrinkled white skin and oozing clear fluid. He had not been able to keep up with his group and was sitting beside the Humane Borders water station, hoping that eventually he could get help from someone.

Luis wanted to go back home and had asked some Humane Borders volunteers to call the Border Patrol. The volunteers gave him a migrant food pack: a plastic bag filled with granola bars, peanuts, and a can of tuna. They refilled his water bottle and promised to call the Border Patrol. When I saw him I wondered where the yellow soccer shirt came from. He surely did not travel all the way from the border wearing that. Maybe he scavenged it from one of the rest areas where migrants sleep. It probably had been left behind when a group was picked up by either their coyote or the Border Patrol.

Luis slowly made his way to the paved road, limping on his blistered feet. Three Border Patrol vehicles passed by at different times, but none stopped.

Luis's story is a textbook case of circular migration. Historically, migration in the Southwest has been from south to north, extending

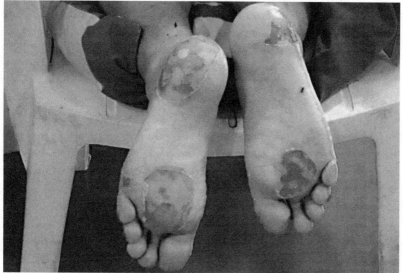

Photograph by Norma Price

Blistered feet, a common medical condition from walking in desert.

back before Europeans ever came to the New World. During the latter half of the twentieth century circular patterns emerged as people in need of work came north to the United States for employment. They returned to their homes in Mexico or Central America for holidays, weddings, and funerals and then journeyed back to the United States to continue in their jobs. In Guatemala Luis had for years worked picking coffee beans. Then the farm where he was employed was sold to an international company. Coffee prices throughout the world plummeted, and the multinational conglomerates, which now owned the coffee *fincas*, paid low wages. His income was no longer able to support his family. To supplement his earnings he grew a few vegetables and sold them in his wife's small *tienda*. In this little store she sold a few notions: shampoo and soap, hair ribbons, combs and brushes, feminine products, a few candies, peanuts, and sodas. Over on the side of her one-room store were the vegetables that Luis grew.

Luis told us he was on the way to Mesa, Arizona, a suburb of Phoenix, where he went every year to pick lettuce. There he earned eight dollars an hour. He sent money home every two weeks and saved the rest. When lettuce-picking season was over, he used the savings to buy counterfeit identification cards so he could travel across the country at less risk of apprehension. With ID in hand he boarded a bus in Mesa bound for North Carolina where he picked tobacco and earned ten dollars an hour. During the tobacco-growing season he would earn $2,000 to $3,000, which he would take home to Guatemala. There in the city he would buy items for his wife's tienda, and with the remainder of the money purchase seeds and seedlings for vegetables to grow and sell. To keep his job at the coffee finca, several days' travel from his community, he hired others to harvest the vegetables that he planted. The next season he would travel again to Arizona to pick lettuce and thus continue the cycle of travel, labor, and hope.

There has been south-to-north migration in this southwestern territory for hundreds of years. People from Mexico and farther south have commuted to the United States for jobs since the end of the Mexican-American War in 1848. Even prior to that time, the Spanish as well as indigenous people moved south to north; families traveled back and forth in this region for purpose of commerce, celebrations, and work. In Arizona, the southern U.S. border bisected the land of the Tohono O'odham people, dividing families into Mexican or U.S. inhabitants. Members of the Tohono O'odham Nation continually moved back and forth for family occasions, for trading, ceremonies, and political events. They did not recognize the border because it had no importance in their lives.

In the 1880s, the Southern Pacific Railroad was built through southern Arizona. The railroad, the mining industry, a large investment of capital, and a water reclamation project resulted in a surge of population. All of these enterprises needed labor from Mexico. Before the twentieth century there were no restrictions on entry into the United States. Even after ports of entry were established, there was no strict control and people from both sides of the border commuted back and forth.

My friend Moises tells of problems that affected lettuce growers in Yuma, Arizona. For years migrants have crossed the border unhindered to pick lettuce during season. Now because of political pressure there has been firmer border control. The fields were full of rotting lettuce. A million dollars of crops were reported lost. After calls and arrangements were made, suddenly the lettuce pickers were back in the fields. Laborers could be seen crossing around the edge of the border wall in their work clothes, no attempt to detain them. The United States needs migrant labor.

Luis's feet healed. I suppose he returned to Guatemala. Maybe he was able to continue his odyssey and harvest the lettuce that I ate in my salad at lunch today. I do know he is a survivor, that our country needs his labor and that of his fellow paisanos, and that we will continue to enjoy the fruits of their hard work.

Ted

Previous page: View of border wall from Nogales, Mexico.

Story Thirty-seven

It is 5:00 a.m. and I am wide awake, having tossed and turned all night waiting for this hour so I can arise. The ride home will be a mouthful of yawns for me. I am returning to Sasabe and Ladrillal, the brickyard. Three vehicles, six other people, and twice the amount of supplies as last time will accompany me.

I arrive at the shed, and we begin to load the two trucks that will cross into Sasabe. My full-size Chevy and another mid-sized Nissan are soon filled to the brim with supplies, including 150 plastic rosaries that our party will use to smooth our way with the coyotes. They will think we are with the church and won't restrict our access to the migrants.

It takes a lot of energy and time to gather the supplies, and one in our group has done most of the work without much help. I had picked up sixty pounds of supplies the day before, but she had done the brunt of the work. I have never given much thought to how the supplies come to be in the shed. They are always there and we never run out of anything, but the gathering of water, food, and medical supplies requires a tremendous effort by people I never see or hear of. Many churches donate time, money, and materials to keep this line of supplies stocked. Without their work we in the field would be reduced to driving around the desert offering Lifesavers and bubble gum.

Our little caravan heads south toward the border. We are a mixed bag of experienced Samaritans and first-timers. One in our group is a big Mexican American guy who wears sunglasses and looks like he would be perfect as a bouncer at a bar. I'm glad he is along, since we're a large group and we will need to keep an eye on each other.

We arrive in Sasabe and park near the general store on the U.S. side. The three people following in the car climb into the bed of my truck. Their car has no Mexican insurance, and though we are going only five miles in, if you do get in an accident it can be difficult to get your car and your self back across the border without it.

Two hundred feet south of the cattle guard that serves as a boundary with Mexico is the *aduana*, or customs house. This is a different sort of Samaritan work. We are not sponsored by any Mexican organization and are not protected by any official designation such as Red Cross or the Catholic Church. We are simply U.S. citizens doing humanitarian work in a foreign country. We tell the customs officer we are giving supplies to Grupo Beta so as to keep the red tape at a minimum. I worry that one day a customs officer is going to ask Grupo Beta what they are doing with all the supplies we are supposedly giving them and then we are going to get some grief. There is a green bag on the front seat of my truck and the official asks to look in it. It appears a pistol would fit in it nicely. It is full of medical supplies. The official waves us on through.

We pass through the town and stop at Anparna's house and chat on the porch. The numbers of migrants crossing is way down in this area, and the reasons are not clear. Anparna says the *narcotraficantes*, the drug smugglers, are killing migrants and scaring people off. Contacts in Altar say it's the *federales* blockading the highway in Hermosillo. Border Patrol says it's their stepped-up enforcement. Some Samaritans say it's the natural ebb and flow of human migration or the recent national elections. Whatever the reasons, the border is two thousand miles long, and if migrants are not here it only means they are crossing somewhere else.

We continue south toward the brickyard, and fifteen minutes later we arrive. A truck piled high with mesquite firewood is pulling out, and we slow down. The man driving yells, "Hey, they've come back!" I consider this a good omen; at least they recognize us as friends.

The place looks the same as last time, a graveyard of Ford trucks and vans in various states of decomposition and small houses built with red burnt adobe brick. There is one thing different, however. The big kiln across from the tienda we had parked at last time has a fresh load of bricks stacked up in the sun. I was under the impression they no longer made bricks here, but I was wrong.

We spread a big tarp down by the truck next to the road and put out the supplies. Our first customers are the children who live in the brickyard. I recognize some of them from the last trip down, a ragtag group of barefoot kids. We have brought a few tennis shoes that will fit the little ones, and they line up to be outfitted. We don't have near enough of the small sizes, but we do the best we can, and eventually some of the small children are running around in shoes with rolled down big-people socks.

A pickup full of migrants heads toward the border.

The first van of the day arrives, towed by another truck. Obviously it broke down on that bone-jarring ninety-one-kilometer journey from Altar, a common occurrence given the condition of the road and the testimony of all the hulks of vehicles strewn about the landscape. One of our group approaches the van, an outstretched arm laden with plastic rosaries. The men inside take the rosaries. A short man with sandals takes two. He is wearing a big gold chain with a replica of an AK-47 in gold around his neck.

This man is not a migrant. Later he hangs around our tarp, sitting in the bed of a pickup, and now he has six rosaries. We take five of them back. The short man is busy, and throughout the day he brings single migrants from some other place on foot to the tienda across the street. He is always talking and explaining something and seems to know everyone.

Men gather around an outdoor kitchen where an older woman has food cooking. We reiterate who we are and that the goods are free, and soon the men wander over in groups of two or three. Everyone takes at least two bottles of water, food, and socks. Some men need shoes. One man put the shoes he had been wearing, a fairly decent pair of black slip-on loafers completely unsuitable for walking in the desert back down on the tarp. He gestures to us, letting us know he is giving up his dress shoes for anyone who might need them.

I ask a small boy to help me carry a bench seat from a gutted van over to a sliver of shade next to my truck and sit down. Many of the neighbors are starting to show up and begin picking through our supplies. These people are not migrants and seem to be getting a little greedy. We put the kibosh on the grabbing of five pairs of socks and filling plastic bags with food.

A van arrives. This one has some women in it. We hand them bags that contain extra food and water, socks, and sanitary napkins.

Another van arrives. The driver does not allow the occupants out of the vehicle; so we reach in and pass out the goods to the occupants. This van has large packages stuffed under the seats filled with what appears to be marijuana, and the migrants will not leave their seats. They are probably responsible for this cargo and fear the consequences of leaving it unattended.

I am told that a young man has an eye injury. I go and get my medical bag and take a look at it. He has a series of nasty gashes over and around his left eye that have been sewn up with what looks like fishing line. He says he saw a doctor the day after it happened. He claims a drunk on the U.S. side struck him with a beer bottle, and it looks like it. I give him some antiseptic swabs and tell him to keep it clean and to please go back to his doctor in a few days.

We are introduced to a young man named Tito who is with his wife. She tells us that he has eighteen *pollos*, seven of them women, and offers to bring them to the *tienda gratis* (free store). They arrive in the back of his pickup truck. One young girl is wearing a pink halter-top and jeans with sequins glued on. She looks like she's going shopping at the mall, not walking in the desert, which is what she'll be doing shortly. Another woman looks like a professor of literature, her face intelligent and inquiring but also very tense, her upcoming border crossing causing anxiety that is easy to read.

Another van empties, and I am called over to look at a boy who looks thirteen but says he is eighteen. Someone thinks he looks pale and ill. I don't. He has chewing gum on his clothes and the back of his head and looks like he just woke up from a nap. He has probably done what children do—fall asleep with gum in their mouth and it ends up stuck on clothes and hair. I think he is just embarrassed at having gum all over himself. I give him some concentrated vitamin C with electrolytes and tell him to drink it. I'm not skilled enough to do anything else. He claims he is fine. The man watching over him says he is just nervous because this is his first time trying to cross.

One of our volunteers gives a lecture about the hardship and the dangers the migrants will face. She tells them it's a five-day walk to Tucson and three to Arivaca. The *pollero* thinks this is misleading, and he gathers his pollos around him after she finishes. Just out of our earshot, he talks emphatically to his little group. We cannot hear what he is saying, but I imagine he wants to refute the amount of walking she said they were in for. Drawing timelines that interfere with the coyotes may cause some unwanted problems. My concern is that we want to remain in the good graces of this operation.

The brickyard is obviously a place that is outside the law: narcotics and human cargo come through here, and it is not a place you want to trifle with or make enemies of any kind. So it is a fine line we dance along, and that line continually moves and shimmies and shakes. You have to keep your head up. One volunteer notices two men loitering behind her truck. They are in a near stupor, just swaying and staring into her cab. She says hello and there is no response. Whatever drug they are on, it has made them zombielike. She calls the big Mexican American with sunglasses over, and the sight of him sends the two scurrying away.

A police truck pulls up to the tienda and parks. I have seen cops in Sasabe, but never out here, and they always make me nervous no matter where I see them. Federales are scarier, and the regular army guys are most scary of all. Very quickly I realize this dread I'm feeling is exactly how a migrant must feel as soon as he crosses the border. There are two officers in the bed of the truck and two in the cab. They carry automatic weapons. The cops go into the tienda and come out ten minutes later without even acknowledging us. We do not exist, which is fine by me.

Another van arrives. This one is carrying a light load: three children and three men. The boy is maybe nine years old. He is traveling with his older brother, who is in his twenties, and two young sisters. The other two men are not related to the group and are probably the guides. The younger girl is behaving strangely. She is not dressed appropriately for travel in the desert—black velour pants and a pink short-sleeve pullover cotton shirt—but that is not unusual. It is the heavy brow, pudgy small frame, and aimless behavior. We ask the oldest man in her group, and he confirms our fears. She is mentally retarded, wets herself, and generally has a hard time controlling her emotions and behavior. This innocent will be crossing over a landscape that kills over two hundred people a year in the Tucson Sector alone, and what can I do? I can only try and make her laugh by teaching her to say "hot dog" instead of *salchicha* as I prepare a meal from military field rations. She giggles as I teach her to sound out the word. It is all I have left to offer. The madness I am witnessing, this absurd carnival of life moving inexorably north, has no boundaries. I offer my prayers and some little comforts. It is all I can do. There is no border here. These are people, just like me.

The drive back to Tucson is in the heat of the day, and my air conditioner is not working. Not much is said, and my heart is heavy. Seven days later a doctor in Sells, Arizona, reports that an eleven-year-old migrant had been brought into the hospital. They tried to revive her, but it was too late. Her older sister was deported immediately. The two had been picked up west of the Baboquivari Mountains on the Indian reservation less than twenty-five miles as the crow flies from Sasabe. Their guide had left them in the desert.

I am heartsick. Is this the retarded girl I saw? I call the attending physician. It is an awkward phone call as I try to suss the doctor out. I am told she was very upset at the loss of life, and I can tell that she does not want to describe the child. I describe to her what the girl looked like in Sasabe. She asks if the child I saw had long hair to the middle of her back and pink tennis shoes. No. Her hair was just past her shoulders and her shoes brown. This is enough to confirm we are dealing with two different little girls, and no more descriptions are given nor asked. I thank her for her time and hang up.

Whatever sense of relief I feel is bitter. The little girl whose face smiled at me in Sasabe may as well be the dead long-haired girl the doctor tried to save. They are all a part of me and of each other.

Story Thirty-eight

Today was different. I traveled alone. I traveled to some places I had not been before. I went to a hill off Brown Canyon with a sign that says, "Vehicles prohibited beyond this point." That doesn't keep the Border Patrol from climbing up to the crest in their vehicles. I drove up. And of course it was obvious. You can see every thing for 360 degrees for a long way. It's a perfect place to perch when you want to see things like migrants or mules or Samaritans or whatever.

I saw deer. I saw things I could not identify through my field glasses. A little piece of red under a tree a quarter mile away. A truck way over about a half a mile, just sitting under some trees. A hunter? Or the hunted? I did not investigate.

Mule deer moving, ever moving. They don't stop, can't stop. All of this on a windswept hill under the watchful eye of Baboquivari Peak, the sentinel whose eye is not only the beacon and guide to migrants who walk the trails north but also the beginning of all beginnings for the native people who have lived in the area for a lot longer than others of us. When the sun comes up and places his red warmth on the eastern flank of its countenance, you can know inside of your heart that you have witnessed something that has guided many people and given them a sense of place in this wide country for many, many years.

Most of the tracks are a day old. Cutting sign, the Border Patrol had dragged the dirt road with large tires, erasing old footprints so that newer ones would show. The migrants keep moving if they can. I would too. I did find three, though, between mileposts 18 and 19. One had wrenched his knee and could hardly walk. They were from Acapulco. They wanted to go back to Sasabe, where they had crossed, and then go home. They asked for a ride, but I said it wasn't possible, "It's against the law." "La pinche migra," one of them said.

The one who had wrenched his knee had a huge belly, like he drank a lot. I thought, no wonder he twisted something. It's amazing they got eighteen miles into the country with him. The other two were in a little better shape for the desert. One was young and very slight with a wispy mustache. The other was thick and had a bunch of silver teeth. They were in relatively good spirits because they had been walking only twenty-four hours, and the high temperature was only eighty or so. Heat wouldn't kill them, but the cold after the sun went down might.

I drove to Sasabe and called it in on 911 and then returned to their location just as the Border Patrol officer arrived; a young Latino man, all macho, with shades. The three were no longer there.

I said to him, "I called it in, sir, told them to wait for you or me." He looked at me coldly. I went on: "Apparently someone picked them up, cuz the one dude was not walking anywhere—his knee was pretty messed up."

The agent turned away from me in disgust and began walking toward his truck. Why was he pissed at me? I was just trying to help. It could mean only two things to me. Someone had picked them up and headed south to return them to the border without having to deal with "la pinche migra," or someone had picked them up and headed north. Either way this agent wasn't going to be able to arrest them.

Story Thirty-nine

We Must Control Our Border," screams the headline in the local paper (*Arizona Daily Star*, Saturday, July 22, 2006). So says Dennis Hastert, Speaker of the U.S. House of Representatives, who is in the area setting up photo ops and grazing the media for his reelection. The present administration's quest for a "comprehensive immigration bill" has driven the Speaker to come down to the border and take a look-see for himself. I ask myself, "How can you clamp off two thousand miles of border?" You can't. The migrants will come as long as the forces are in place that draw them.

It is in the middle of summer, a time of intense heat and humidity. The daily formation of clouds portends rain. Sometimes it arrives. Three of us head out at 5:00 a.m. One of my companions is new to this work, while the other has been with the organization for years.

We decide to head south on Route 286 and see if there is any sign of migrants on the trails that hug the eastern flank of the Baboquivari Range. Reports are that very few migrants have been seen in this area. In the past these trails were a major route for entering the United States, but since the National Guard has shown up they have gone relatively quiet.

About a mile and a half from the border we head west on a dirt road and drive for a while. We cross a number of trails and see no signs of traffic. We pass a fairly large building that has no windows. A chain-link fence with razor wire surrounds it. There are no identifying signs or symbols anywhere to let one know what this building is used for. My companion says it's "Homeland Security stuff." Her guess is as good as any.

We continue west and eventually reach the low hills that announce the beginning of the Baboquivaris, and here we see the National Guard camp. It sits on a hill with a commanding view of the area, a camouflaged tent blending so well into the surrounding desert we would have missed it if we had not been so close to it. The president of the United States has called for six thousand Guard troops to be deployed along the border, and this is the first contingent I have seen.

We drive past and turn around at a no-trespassing sign. On the way back to the highway we see two more of these camps, which we had missed coming in, and pass a National Guard convoy of Humvees. We wave.

We head north on the paved road and go west again on a ranch road about six miles north of the border. Again no sign of any recent activity. High above us jets engage in mock dogfights, releasing flares that look like missiles. They scream away.

We go into the visitors' center on the Buenos Aires National Wildlife Refuge and talk to the ranger on duty. She is very friendly. She tells us she lives out here and her house has been broken into three times. Her boss is going to put a chain-link fence with razor wire around her house, and she is upset about it. It is a beautiful place to live, and the migrants only take food when they break in. She doesn't want the fence. She tells us the refuge shares five and a half miles of border with Mexico and in that space there are 160 trails that cut north. She says the original fence between the countries is nonexistent. It was only barbed wire and was used to keep the Mexican cattle out. Now a new barbed-wire fence maintained by the government is set up about a mile and a half north of the border. No one is allowed south past that fence without armed law enforcement as escort.

We continue into the town of Arivaca and stop by my friend's house. His girlfriend tracks jaguars; this area of Arizona is famous for them. The outfit she works for tracks the sign and tries to get pictures of the beautiful spotted animals in Arizona. She uses automatic cameras that are set off by heat sensors at night or day. Sometimes she gets pictures of startled migrants, but sometimes those who don't want their pictures taken destroy the cameras. The cats could care less about the border and have huge ranges, hundreds of miles on either side. They are migrants that will travel wherever they need to for food.

We ask him to join us for lunch at a taco stand. In town one of the locals approaches us. She has seen three young travelers who were in need of food and water. They had walked off in the direction of the wash. We split into two groups and began searching using walkie-talkies to stay in touch.

In fifteen minutes the other two found one of the migrants, a Guatemalan named Reyes. His two companions, he said, were nearby. He sits under a big cottonwood in tears. He had used the phone in town to call for a pickup, but their contact was having car trouble and told him to call back in two hours. They have been walking for two days.

Reyes wants to know if there is a hotel nearby so they can rest and take a shower. He then offers to buy a car for seven hundred dollars. He isn't making a lot of sense, and I'm worried he is too exhausted to make a sound decision.

We sit with him for half an hour as he eats our food and drinks water. Eventually he asks for enough supplies to walk up to Tucson. From there he can contact someone to give them a ride.

He had crossed over one other time and walked for six days in the desert before being picked up by a coyote in Eloy, Arizona. He had spent three years working in North Carolina before returning home to visit family, and now he wanted to go back to work. This time he was crossing without the use of a guide, and he was responsible for the other two.

My friend in Arivaca says he will come back later that evening with a big bucket of water and soap so they can wash up, along with some hot food. We leave supplies for Luis and go back to the truck. A Border Patrol agent drives by, and we smile and wave hello.

We head home. The next day I contact my friend in Arivaca. He said that about two hours later he went to the post office and saw Reyes walking down the road in a different shirt. Reyes smiled and waved to him. Later that evening he dropped off water, soap, and food under the big cottonwood tree, but when he checked back the next morning it had not been touched.

Cross memorializing death of sixty-four-year-old migrant whose body was found by Green Valley Samaritans.

Homage

~ Kathryn

IN MEMORY OF REMAINS DISCOVERED BY HUMANITARIANS:
LUCRESIA DOMINGUEZ LUNA, FOUND JULY 2005; PRUDENCIA MARTIN GOMEZ,
FOUND JULY 2007; JOSSELINE JAMILETH HERNANDEZ, FIFTEEN YEARS OLD,
FOUND FEBRUARY 2008; ALFONSO SALIS VILLAGRAN, A SIXTY-FOUR-YEAR-OLD
MAN WHOSE BODY WAS FOUND AUGUST 2006 ONE HUNDRED YARDS FROM
A ROAD. AND IN MEMORY OF ALL OTHERS.

We walk the remote trail, heads bent into hot wind, following footprints blowing to memory. Prints skim the surface of the earth like a blanket of parched stars fallen from a burning sky.

We move into desert, mesmerized by moon dust sand that shines like ground glass. No human lives here. Two thousand square miles of scorched land.

A coiled wind slaps our faces. We inch forward looking through eyelashes. Diving air obliterates Anasazi trails of those who came before, leaving only whispers to guide us.

The backpack lies on a pockmarked stone. Nearby is the dark body with skin like stretched leather. In a rumpled pile lies a shirt that bit into her like a thousand red army ants, ripped off in the last hours of life. One shoe is here, one is there. Near her foot, a cracked plastic jug caked in brown with the last sip of her own urine. Inside the backpack, a toothbrush, a bus ticket from Mexico City to Hermosillo, a photo of a man, a woman, and a boy.

We sit by the corpse. A dust devil spins toward us. It knocks back my head, my arms, filling my mouth, coating my tongue. Sand blows across the face of the dead woman, through the eye sockets. It covers the body, covers the dream.

She walked forward with hope, but on the backside of a promise unkept she died alone. We return to the truck to call. Men arrive from the coroner's office, miles away. They stretch neon-blue surgical gloves over fat fingers, place the traveler in a body bag, shove her onto a shelf of a white van, drive away, and we are left standing in the wind looking down at six blue gloves tossed in the sand.

Photograph by Kathryn Ferguson

Tin art on Mexico side of border wall by Alfred Quiróz, Alberto Morackis, and Guadalupe Serrano.

Epilogue

We keep learning. At the end of each day on the trail, we return home overloaded with new experiences. We have learned that it doesn't stop. Migration historically has been an integral part of the borderlands and still is. But, primarily, what we have learned is that the deaths in the desert result from a clash between the past and the present. A clash between an old restrictive way of thinking and a new inclusive reality.

As with countries throughout the world, our culture is a product of all others. We see this in foreign goods we happily purchase in the markets, in scientific information discovered by the best minds from multiple nations, in the food we eat, in our multicultural arts and sports, in the people that walk our streets. Our culture is mixed; the word "immigrant" doesn't apply. Even during raids on the workplace by the U.S. government, officials end up apprehending people who are legal residents because officials can't tell the difference. It is currently reported that one out of five U.S. citizens has a grandparent who came here from another country.

The problem is bigger than the question, "If vegetables can cross the border, why can't humans?" It is bigger than NAFTA, the agreement that permits U.S. corporations to undersell Mexican corn and sugarcane, causing loss of livelihood to Mexican farmers. It is bigger than building a $400 billion wall. It is bigger than immigration reform. It is bigger than a change of policies between the U.S. and Mexican governments.

The problem is that the deaths on our Arizona desert are a result of a suffocating, nonfunctioning concept of "my world is better than your world." This anachronistic thinking creates our last-ditch effort to keep people out of the United States by constructing military resistance to control a socioeconomic shift that has already occurred. Nation-states are a thing of the past. There is mass migration throughout the world as people from Africa enter Italy and Spain, Turks enter Germany, and those from Tajikistan look for work in Russia. On our U.S.–Mexican border, a wall that is medieval in structure and concept is no more than a speed bump in slowing migration from Mexico and Central and South America.

We have learned here in our border community that aid from humanitarian groups is strong and is built individual by individual. People give by spending time on the desert, working to change unjust laws, or donating money. The Tohono O'Odham, whose land was divided by the international line, historically have helped people on both sides of the line. Arizona Latinos were giving support long before Anglo humanitarian groups were formed.

We have learned that migration is not going away. We are now an internationally technologically savvy generation of people with a share-information mentality. This information-sharing activity eliminates and creates new boundaries that are not drawn on traditional world maps. To name a few changes, the new world "map" is comprised of globalization (created by individual and societal technological interaction), new forms of transportation, and communication such as satellite television, GPS tracking—so common that we have it in our pets—and instant Internet information. By letting go of the notion of nation-states, these changes create a different "map" of the world with no borderlines as we have known them, making a more interdependent world.

With twentieth-century medical advancements setting the stage for an unparalleled population explosion, the high-speed exchange of personal and impersonal information, and new abilities to travel, the powerful waves of migration we now witness are not going away. Migration in many forms is here to stay.

Perhaps these massive technological connections will bring solutions. Survival on this small planet carries a mandate for cooperation, tolerance, and a multilateral approach to the resolution of international conflict. With this tectonic shift in communication and global thinking, we create new ways to balance the need for international community against the old battleground of individual desire. We are in the process of creating a bridge across the no-man's land of political polarization. The fences of isolationism no longer serve. Inclusive, solution-based thinking is a far cry from solving international problems with a fifteen-foot-tall metal wall.

ॐ ॐ

Further Reading and Resources

Web Sites

www.samaritanpatrol.org
www.nomoredeaths.org

Reading Recommendations

Baca, Jimmy Santiago. *Thirteen Mexicans*. New York: Grove Press, 2002.
Bowden, Charles. *Chihuahua: Pictures from the Edge*. Albuquerque: University of New Mexico Press, 1996.
————. *Juárez: The Laboratory of Our Future*. New York: Aperture, 1998.
Cabeza de Vaca, Álvar Núñez. *Cabeza de Vaca's Adventures in the Unknown Interior of America*. Translated and edited by Cyclone Covey. Albuquerque: University of New Mexico Press, 1983.
Chomsky, Aviva. *"They Take Our Jobs!": And 20 Other Myths about Immigration*. Boston: Beacon Press, 2007.
Conover, Ted. *Coyotes: A Journey through the Secret World of America's Illegal Aliens*. New York: Vintage Books, 1987.
Crosthwaite, Luis Humberto, John William Byrd, and Bobby Byrd, with Jessica Powers, eds. *Puro Border: Dispatches, Snapshots, and Graffiti*. El Paso, TX: Cinco Puntos Press, 2003.
Davidson, Miriam. *Convictions of the Heart: Jim Corbett and the Sanctuary Movement*. Tucson: University of Arizona Press, 1988.
Díaz del Castillo, Bernal. *The Conquest of New Spain*. Translated by J. M. Cohen. Baltimore: Penguin Books, 1963.
Ganster, Paul, and David E. Lorey. *The U.S.–Mexican Border into the Twenty-first Century*. Lanham, MD: Rowman and Littlefield, 2008.
Gershten, Donna. *Kissing the Virgin's Mouth*. New York: HarperCollins, 2001.
Gilb, Dagoberto. *Gritos*. New York: Grove Press, 2003.
Gómez Peña, Guillermo. *The New World Border: Prophecies, Poems, and Loqueras for the End of the Century*. San Francisco: City Lights, 1996.
Gonzalez, Juan. *Harvest of Empire: A History of Latinos in America*. New York: Viking, 2000.
Guskin, Jane, and David L. Wilson. *The Politics of Immigration: Questions and Answers*. New York: Monthly Review Press, 2007.

Herrera, Juan Felipe. *187 Reasons Mexicanos Can't Cross the Border: Undocuments, 1971–2007*. San Francisco: City Lights, 2007.

Martínez, Demetria. *Mother Tongue*. Tempe, AZ: Bilingual Press/Editorial Bilingüe, 1994.

Nazario, Sonia. *Enrique's Journey*. New York: Random House, 2006.

Nevins, Joseph. *Dying to Live: A Story of U.S. Immigration in an Age of Global Apartheid*. San Francisco: Open Media/City Lights Books, 2008.

————. *Operation Gatekeeper: The Rise of the "Illegal Alien" and the Making of the U.S.–Mexico Boundary*. New York: Routledge, 2002.

Urrea, Luis Alberto. *Across the Wire: Life and Hard Times on the Mexican Border*. New York: Anchor Books, 1993.

————. *By the Lake of Sleeping Children: The Secret Life of the Mexican Border*. New York: Anchor Books, 1996.

————. *The Devil's Highway*. Boston: Little, Brown, 2004.

Film/Video

De Nadie. Directed by Tin Dirdamal. Mexico: Producciones Tranvía, 2005.

Dying to Get In: Undocumented Immigration at the U.S.–Mexican Border. Directed by Brett Tolley. USA: Mooncusser Films, 2005.

Invisible Chapel. Directed by John Carlos Frey. Gatekeeper Productions, n.d.

Invisible Mexicans of Deer Canyon. Directed by John Carlos Frey. Gatekeeper Productions, 2006.

Señorita Extraviada (Missing Young Woman). Directed by Lourdes Portillo. Mexico, 2001.

About the Authors

KATHRYN FERGUSON is a dancer, choreographer, and independent film-maker. She studied modern and ethnic dance and music in the United States, Morocco, and Cairo. She teaches dance at her studio in Tucson, Arizona. She has toured and performed in eleven countries, including Germany, the Netherlands, Australia, Turkey, and Mexico. As a filmmaker, she has produced dance videos that are available internationally. After traveling much of her life in Mexico and spending years in Chihuahua's Sierra Madre, she produced and directed two feature-length award-winning documentaries, *The Unholy Tarahumara* and *Rita of the Sky*. She worked in media for PBS KUAT-TV for four years. As a native Tucsonan, she has had a lifelong concern and love for the borderlands. Since the year 2004, she has volunteered with Samaritans to work in the desert to prevent deaths.

TED PARKS became involved with the Samaritan movement in the fall of 2005. He worked in the restaurant industry for twenty years, including eight years as the owner of a restaurant in Tucson, Arizona. He is a member of the Screen Actors Guild and has appeared in numerous film and television roles. A founding member of the Theatre of N.O.T.E., he attended the University of California, Irvine, and has produced, directed, or acted in over fifty plays. He continues to witness the travesty of social injustice from the porch of the railroad house near the Nogales line in South Tucson.

NORMA PRICE has lived for over a decade in southern Arizona and has become a true denizen of the desert. Since moving to Tucson, she has embraced Southwest culture, enjoying many outdoor activities and the proximity to Mexico. Before moving to Tucson she practiced medicine in Atlanta, Georgia, for twenty-five years.

Norma graduated from the University of Tennessee School of Medicine in Memphis, Tennessee, where she also completed internship and residency in internal medicine, followed by a fellowship in hematology. Subsequent oncology fellowships at M. D. Anderson Hospital in Houston, Texas, and Emory University Hospital and Clinic in Atlanta completed her medical training.

Norma volunteers at a local medical clinic for the uninsured. She remains committed to the work of Samaritans and other humanitarian and activist groups that focus on border issues. She lives with her husband, Stan Windham, in Tucson, Arizona.

About the Contributors

CLAUDIA ABURTO GUZMÁN is an associate professor of Spanish at Bates College, Maine. She focuses on Latin American literatures and cultures, Mexico–U.S. literatures and cultures, and translation differences at the Mexico–U.S. border. Her creative writing has been published by various Spanish-language presses and journals, and her photography and mixed-media projects have been shown in the Tucson Sector of the U.S. borderlands.

JOHN FIFE is the retired pastor of Southside Presbyterian Church in Tucson where he served for thirty-five years. He was cofounder of the Sanctuary Movement in the 1980s and served as the elected leader of the Presbyterian Church (USA) in 1992. He is a founding member of Humane Borders, Samaritans, and No More Deaths, and volunteers with the Raptor Free Flight program at the Arizona-Sonora Desert Museum.